THE KANURI OF BORNO

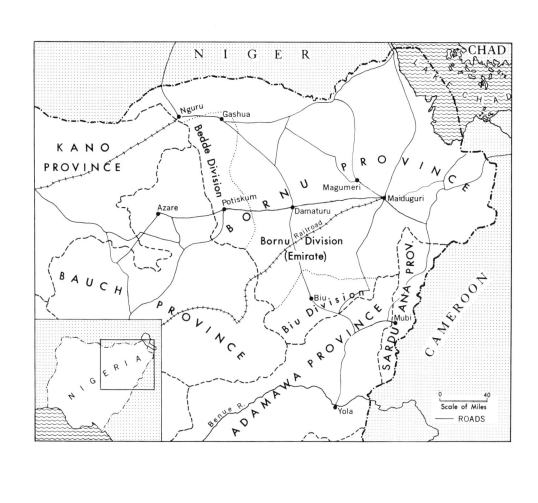

NIGER

CHAD

KANO
PROVINCE

Nguru

Gashua

Bedde Division

BORNU

PROVINCE

Magumeri

Maiduguri

Azare

Potiskum

Damaturu

Railroad

Bornu Division
(Emirate)

SARDUANA PROV.

BAUCHI

PROVINCE

Biu

Biu Division

Mubi

CAMEROON

NIGERIA

ADAMAWA PROVINCE

Benue R.

Yola

0   40
Scale of Miles
—— ROADS

THE KANURI OF BORNO

By

RONALD COHEN
University of Florida

WAVELAND
PRESS, INC.
Prospect Heights, Illinois

For information about this book, write or call:

Waveland Press, Inc.
P.O. Box 400
Prospect Heights, Illinois 60070
(312) 634-0081

Cover: A young wife preparing food.

Foreword

About the Author

Ronald Cohen (Ph.D. Wisconsin 1960) has taught anthropology at the University of Toronto (1958-1961), at McGill University (1961-1963), Northwestern University (1963-1981) and the University of Florida from 1982 to the present. He was Visiting Professor and Chair of Sociology and Anthropology at Ahmadu Bello University, Zaria Nigeria from 1972 to 1974 and a Fellow of the Center for Advanced Study in the Behavioral Sciences, Palo Alto, California (1976-1977). He is interested in problems of social and political change and development in the Third World, as well as issues of theory and method in the social sciences. He has carried out fieldwork in Nigeria, in the Mackenzie Valley, Northwest Territories in Canada and in the bureaucracy at the Department of Commerce, Washington, D.C. From 1977 to 1979 he served on a team of specialists to create the Master Plan for Nigeria's new capital city of Abuja. At the University of Florida, Professor Cohen is a member of the Center for African Studies where he is presently working on problems of food production in Africa. He has written and co-authored a number of books and articles on Africa, Canada and political anthropology, as well as method and theory in the social sciences.

About the Book

This case study has a clear central focus. The author shows us how the various sectors of Kanuri social life build upon and interrelate to the basic unit of Kanuri society, the household organization. He claims the basic theory of their society is not his own but that of the Kanuri themselves as they have tried to explain their society to him. In doing so they continually refer back to the household. The household, or compound, is the basic political unit; groups of households link up to form wards, hamlets, villages, and districts. The economic system is dependent upon the household, since the business of getting a living is organized within it, and households link together through their head men to form larger organizations for the production of goods or for trade. Family life is carried on in the household, and ways of behaving that are acceptable and necessary in Kanuri life are learned there.

The descriptive analysis of these interdependent relationships centering upon the household is far from mechanistic. Though the structural features of groupings and the modal patterns of activities are made very clear, there is a sense of immediacy in their description. Actual behavior is described and vignettes of individuals and their behaviors, relevant to various sectors of life, are included.

This case study is notable in a number of other ways, but particularly in the sense of history conveyed. In a necessarily brief but informative historical sketch the author shows us how the emirate of Bornu, established in the late fifteenth century, survived insurrection, warfare, colonialism, and even today survives within the framework of national independence as a viable social and political entity. The author ends his historical overview with these questions: "Why has Bornu lasted so long in this area? Why has it adapted so well to modern times?" The case study is, in one of its dimensions, an answer to these questions.

GEORGE AND LOUISE SPINDLER

Acknowledgments

The fieldwork on which this book is based has been carried out in two periods: one in 1956 and 1957 under the auspices of the Ford Foundation Area Fellowship Program, and again in the summers of 1964 and 1965 with financial help from the Program of African Studies at Northwestern University, the National Institute of Mental Health, and the National Science Foundation of Washington, D.C. It is because of the generosity of these agencies that I have been able to develop and continue my understanding of the Kanuri people and their complex culture. Altogether I have spent over twenty-six months among the Kanuri and a number of years reading historical documents dealing with their pre-colonial kingdom in the Chad basin.

Over the years I have become indebted to a host of people who have contributed to my expanding knowledge of Bornu so that it would be impossible to give a complete list of those whose share in this book is a significant one. Professor C. W. M. Hart first encouraged and guided my work, and his approach to anthropology has colored and given direction to my own. In Nigeria, Sir Kashim Ibrahim, G.C.O.N., K.C.M.G., C.B.E., LL.B., Governor of Northern Nigeria, has through the years helped to make my visits to Bornu fruitful and intellectually exciting. The Bornu Native Authority and the Bornu Provincial Government have extended the warmest hospitality and courtesy to myself and my wife and encouraged us in our work. Their forbearance with my research and their constant willingness to cooperate has helped to make Bornu into what some of them have called "my second home." I cannot claim to know everything about Kanuri society and culture; what I have learned is due not only to the kindness of Bornu officials but to the friendship of hundreds of Kanuri who have never failed to answer my unending questions and sometimes naïve curiosity with patient explanation. Dr. and Mrs. Abraham Rosman who were also out in Bornu in 1957 carrying out field research gave invaluable aid as colleagues interested in many of the same problems. At closer range, both in Bornu during my first field trip, and later after we returned to North America in 1957, my wife has served as a constant critic and discussant of almost every fact and interpretation put forward in this book and in my other publications on Bornu. In a very real way I owe her a debt as my collaborator and fellow researcher. Finally I am indebted to Professor John Middleton and David Spain who have read and made many helpful comments on an earlier draft of this book.

R. C.

Evanston, Illinois
November 1966

Preface, 1986

This book was written two decades ago. Much of the ethnographic material is still relevant and accurate particularly for rural areas. In the urban areas, change and migration from Chad, Niger, and other parts of the country have made the population more heterogeneous. Rural village life goes on much as before. As always, it responds to the forces of climate, soil, local events and especially to the cultural traditions handed down and sometimes adapted over the lifetimes of the peoples of Borno.

The original title of the book, *The Kanuri of Bornu* requires two caveats. First, the geographic area of Bornu, spelled that way since the 1820s, has been changed by the State Government to 'Borno.' Kanuri scholars believe this is a more accurate rendition of its pronunciation. For matters of convenience, the spelling in the text has been left the same. Readers should realize that Borno is now the official spelling of the Kanuri homeland. Secondly, although I do not use the term Bornuan (now Bornoan), it must be understood that the Kanuri comprise only one segment of historical and modern Borno. A plethora of other ethnic groups also call Borno their home. Borno State, represented by all of its diverse peoples, is a significant political and cultural influence in modern Nigeria. In this sense, the term "Bornoan" is an emergent identity just as Texan, Californian, or Floridian has been in the USA.

The village of Magumeri where I did my first field work is typical of many rural towns. Upon our return in the 1980s, many of the same families were still living similar lives as during our original research. The calabash makers, the butchers and the traders are still there. Ajimi the kola-nut seller (see page 89) has left and has been lucky enough to obtain a farm-plot in the new irrigation scheme south of Lake Chad. Mechanization and two cash crops a year have increased farm incomes in that area as much as five times the average for Borno farmers. The public buildings of the town and its layout are much as before, but the population has grown. The south arm of the U-shaped village now reaches out past a row of new cement block houses doubling the former length. At the end there is a fine paved road rather than the sand tracks we found when we first arrived in the 1950s. Local vans and privately owned small buses shuttle people into the city in one hour. Previously the trip required half a day or more in the wet season before the road was built. The little two room primary school has now doubled in size. On the north side of town in an area which used to be a cattle run, there is a post primary school teacher training college for women. On the south side just outside the town, there are two modern bungalows which house agricultural employees. The nearby corrugated iron warehouse announces Magumeri to be a Farm Service Center for the district with resident extension workers. A large water tower, tank, and the machinery for rural electrification, bespeak "development."

Glancing around the town, however, one sees much more that appears to be the same. Mud and grass mat walled compounds are still the rule. Women still go to the well to draw water, or to a pipe stand if the new water tower and its pump are working. The rhythm of life including farm and non-farm activities, market days, the local district court where interesting gossip-making stories circulate and the interactions among people seem familiar and continuous with times past.

The core idea or thesis of the book stressed households as the most important units of organization and the basis for a moral idiom that justified and defined social relations. This theme was somewhat out of step with African anthropology at the time. In the 1940s and 1950s kinship and descent systems (genealogically determined relationships to which people are allocated for purposes of inheritance, memberships, and access to important resources) in particular were deemed the key to understanding local village life in rural Africa. I was trained to observe and record such systems, the activities they encompass and the beliefs associated with them. I did so and kinship *is* an important quality of Kanuri life. As the work unfolded, it became obvious that *households* were the truly central focus of social life. Sometimes they were linked by kinship to one another or by kinlike relations of patronage, occupation, friendship, etc. Nevertheless, every household was always an ongoing political, economic and legal entity in relation to the rest of the society. Wives sold cooked foods on their own, sons might have their own farm plots, children might help a kinsman in a nearby household, but the bulk of economic and social activity was organized and directed within the household.

Marriages are still extremely brittle. In 1971, I published *Dominance and Defiance* about Kanuri divorce. Again, the household was the central focus of the analysis. Divorce does occur in well over half of all marriages and rises much higher in the main cities. Yet, households provide a secure and durable setting for children and for integrating individuals into the wider community.

More recently, I have returned to an interest in households. After a project on the origins of the state among the Bura peoples and a stint helping to plan the new capital city of Nigeria, I am presently working on a third Kanuri book. The focus will be on problems of food production and the capacity of Borno farmers to grow enough food to meet the needs of the rapidly expanding population. Households are the central focus of the research since farming is organized within this unit.

Meanwhile, anthropology has changed. In the 1970s and 1980s anthropologists working in Africa have moved away from kinship and descent as their major or central focus. A new concern for development studies, for data and theory that aim at increased productivity among 'peasant economies' brought households, the locus of production in rural Africa, to center stage. Partly by accident and partly by design, this earlier work is more in line with contemporary approaches and problems than it was at the time of the original writing.

In re-publishing it, I wish to dedicate this volume to the peoples of Borno and to their unfailing kindness and hospitality to me and my family. Over the years they have changed my life, put their stamp on it and given me one of the most rewarding personal experiences I shall ever receive. It is fitting then that this book about them be theirs. For it is.

Ronald Cohen
Nares Inlet

Contents

Foreword   v

Acknowledgements   vii

Preface, 1986   ix

1. The Setting   1

    The Land and the People, 1
    Gathering the Material, 7
    Ethnography and Theory, 11

2. History   12

    Kanem-Bornu: The Historical Background, 12
    Kanem-Bornu: The Social and Political Background, 19
    Pre-nineteenth Century Bornu, 20
    The Nineteenth Century Kingdom, 24
    The Colonial Change, 30

3. The Family and Household in Bornu   33

    The Kinship System, 33
    Married Life, 42
    Other Family Relations and the Behavior Norms, 46
    The Household, 48

4. The Life Cycle: From Birth to Death in Kanuri Society   53

    Gestation, 53
    Birth, 54
    The Naming, 56
    Infancy, 58
    Childhood, 59
    Puberty, 63
    Adolescence, 65
    Maturity, 68
    Old Age, 70
    Death, 72

5. The Economic Life   74

    The Household as an Economic Unit, 75
    Households as Consumers, 76

Households as Producers, 77
Ka'anami, the Calabash Maker, 82
Mala Bukar, the Butcher, 83
Distribution, 85
The Organization of Trade, 88
Momadu, the Salt Seller, 88
Bukar, the Tada Njima, *89*
Ajimi, the Kola Nut Seller, 89
Ajimi's Uncle, 90

6. The Political Organization   92

Households, Wards and Hamlets, 92
The Village Area, 94
The District Organization, 99
The Organization at the Center, 105
Representative Government, 108

7. Conclusion   111

8. Epilogue, 1986   113

Recommended Reading   123

1

The Setting

The Land and the People

F OR AT LEAST a thousand years the drama of empires rising, falling, expanding, and shrinking has been played out in an immense area of Africa at the southern edge of the Sahara known as the Sudan. These states, Ghana, Mali, Songhai, the Hausa kingdoms, Kanem-Bornu, Baghirmi, Wadai, Darfur, and others like them, from the upper Senegal River basin to the upper Nile, form a band from east to west across Africa. Their histories provide some of the most resplendent grandeur of Africa's past. Many of these states have now been consigned to the history books; Ghana and Mali have disappeared although modern countries have resuscitated their names; Songhai was destroyed by the Moroccans at the end of the sixteenth century; the Hausa states were altered as they came under the hegemony of the Fulani Empire of Sokoto at the beginning of the nineteenth century, and little is known as yet about the early states to the east of Lake Chad. On the other hand, Bornu in the northeastern corner of Nigeria has continued its sovereignty in the Chad Basin throughout a millennium of tribulations and triumphs and it goes on today organized as a separate emirate within Bornu Province.

Like most of the Sudan, Bornu is open savannah country, generally quite flat except for a few stable dunes covered with scrub in the north and several long low ridges running northwest to southeast in the southern part of the country. The ridges are probably ancient lake-shores of a great inland sea whose contemporary remnant is Lake Chad—a large shallow fresh water lake into which flow a number of rivers from the south and west. The soil is sandy and covered with scrub bush grass, and scattered trees, mostly thorny ones, except for the large spreading boabab, which dots the horizon here and there. In the 1930s the Nim, a hardy shade tree from India that thrives on the semi-desert conditions of northern Nigeria, was introduced to provide some forest preserves and year round shade in the villages. Here and there, especially at the bottom of the ridges, are large flat surfaces of hard clay that turn into gray-black mud during the rainy season. These provide clay for building materials and pottery, as well as water holes for the cattle of local villages and wandering nomads.

1

The rainfall ranges from twenty-two to twenty-seven inches, in normal years, and is heavier as one moves from north to south. The important point that must be kept sight of is the fact that ninety percent of the rain falls in June, July, August, and September, while the months from October through June are almost totally dry. Indeed even within the four-month rainy season, about eighteen inches of the annual rainfall comes during July and August, so that in exceptionally dry years, June and September can easily turn out to be rainless months.

The various seasons are tied closely to the basic facts of rainfall and latitude. As the rain begins in June the dry sandy soil suddenly comes to life with large stretches of new grass and new leaves on the died-up thorn bushes. From atop one of the Bornu ridges, or from the roof of a house, the entire landscape, as far as the eye can see, starts to change color from yellow-brown to a soft green. The weather cools delightfully, the rains become more frequent, and the short daily storms freshen the air. The people call this period "the rain," and consider it by far the most pleasant time of the year, even though there is extra work for everybody because this is the planting and hoeing season, and there is as well the extra unpleasantness of increased numbers and endless varieties of insects that thrive at this time. After the rains in the months of October and November, and often into mid-December the proximity to the equator produces a short, hot season with clear, still days. In a sense this is autumn. The green of summer fades and the bushland changes to light browns, yellows and grays, except for the ripening millet in the fields, and the evergreen Nim tree. Towards the end of this season the weather cools, and a daily wind from the north to northeast blows in from the Sahara. This is the famous Harmattan that even coats shoreward sides of ships with red dust 100 miles off the coast of West Africa. It starts up about eight o'clock in the morning, to wane by about four in the afternoon, making for relatively cool, still mornings and evenings, with rather harsh, sandy winds, for most of the day, so that one wants to cover face and eyes when riding on horseback, especially into the wind. The people have a special word for this time of year which translates as "winter" but which also means "harvest," since the main crops—millet, guinea corn, and ground-nuts—are harvested towards the end of autumn and beginning of winter. By the end of February or beginning of March the coolness of winter has gone. The Harmattan wind still blows but it gets hotter every day and the nights, although windless and a trifle cooler than the days, begin to approach the daytime temperature. Indeed it is not uncommon for the temperature to remain about 100° F for several weeks on end, so that when a break finally comes, ninety degrees seems like an exuberantly pleasant relief. This is the hot season, called "the heat" locally, and considered by all to be the most unpleasant time of year, which gives even greater sweetness to the cooling rains when they finally arrive in June.

There are, then, in all, four seasons: the rains from June to September; a short, hot season in October and November; a cooler, windy winter from December to February; and a sharply hot dry period from March to June. Another way of looking at the seasons, also used by the people, and one which will be utilized to some extent in this book, is to simply speak of a dry season, from September to June, and a wet season from mid-June to mid-September. Obviously the contrast between the various seasons of the dry months is not nearly so great as between the rainy months and the rest of the year.

(Top) A district head in his reception room; behind him his clients are counting tax returns. The bags on the floor are shillings.

(Bottom) The palace of the Shehu of Bornu.

A naming ceremony—women sitting in front of the mother's hut. (Crowd includes Diana Cohen, wife of the author).

Horsemen saluting a chief in Magumeri.

Today the empire of Bornu is a Muslim emirate, or kingdom, which forms a subdivision of Bornu Province in the northeastern corner of Nigeria. The emirate covers an area of 24,000 square miles and, according to the 1952 census, has a population of about 1 million people of whom 626,000 are Kanuri—the dominant ethnic group of the kingdom. There are also about 160,000 Fulani and Shuwa who tend their cattle in the area and who carry out a semi-nomadic way of life. Another 225,000 people belong to small pagan groups, from south of the province and the Cameroons, as well as from the Hausa-speaking areas to the west and from the other regions of Nigeria. The emirate also includes about 5000 non-Nigerians, who are from Europe, America, the Near East, and other African countries.

Including the emirate, Bornu Province has approximately 1,600,000 people, 750,000 of whom are Kanuri. Thus many Kanuri live outside the political boundaries of the emirate. Indeed Kanuri can be found in all major cities of northern Nigeria in substantial numbers as well as in the neighboring territories of Chad and Niger. In order to identify the population with a particular territory, however, it is convenient to think of the emirate sub-division of Bornu Province as Bornu, the traditional homeland of the Kanuri kingdom. These are the people who are the subject of this book; they describe themselves as "Kanuri—the people of Bornu." As noted above, outside this entity—of Bornu—there are many other Kanuri, and a political entity, Bornu Province. However, these will be referred to by their full names, while the word "Bornu" will be reserved for the political system, whose present expression, the emirate or kingdom, is continuous with the Bornu of precolonial times. This reflects as well the attitude of the people themselves, who use the term "Bornu" to refer primarily to the emirate rather than the larger area of Bornu Province.

One other point should be kept in mind about the population figures. There has been a more recent Nigerian census since 1952, and although the details are unknown as yet, it is generally accepted that the more recent figures are in the neighborhood of thirty-five to forty-five percent higher than those of 1952. This means that Bornu may actually have nearly 900,000 in population, and Bornu Province may reach as high as two million persons, as of 1966.

The Kanuri of Bornu live spread out over the entire area of the emirate, in 306 named and variously sized settlements, ranging from Maiduguri, the capital, with its 80,000 population, down to tiny hamlets of three or four households. Most of the people, about two-thirds of them, live in 248 named village units that range in size from 1000 to 5000. About one-quarter of the population, on the other hand, live in eleven cities whose population is 10,000 or over. This statistical information from the census masks an important point, however, for the towns and villages are really area units and each has within its territory, a set of satellite hamlets that often total to more than half the population of the town or village area. It is this pattern that gives to Bornu its "filled-up" quality even though the population density is approximately twenty-five to forty persons per square mile when calculated from the 1952 census figures or perhaps as much as forty to sixty persons per square mile on the basis of more recent counts. Riding out on horseback into the bush one never feels alone; here and there sprinkled in one or two mile intervals in all directions are little hamlets with their surrounding farmlands while more intermittently, perhaps every five or six miles, are the larger towns and villages. Everyone knows where the boundaries lie between village areas, or between hamlets and other settlements, and there is plenty of land for expansion and for the wandering cattle nomads who traverse the area annually moving their cattle north and south with the coming and going of the rains.

The settlements are all made up of walled compounds and within these are the mud-walled houses with conical thatched roofs, or sometimes grass mat walls with thatched roofs. In the northeast of Bornu the people specialize in a bee-hive shaped house of bound thatch which can be picked up and moved and can reach a size of twenty to thirty feet in diameter, although ten to fifteen feet is more common. A compound is almost always rectangular in shape with mud or grass mat walls and internal partitions. There is only one entrance which is often a house with two doors so that there is a shelter at the doorway for people to gather and visit with the household head. The compounds in any settlement are always arranged in a "U"-shape with the open end towards the west and the closed end on the east. The arms of the U then form the north and south sides of the open plaza where all the major events of town take place. Although in very tiny settlements, big cities, or settlements that have lost a great many people, this U-shape is not often easy to discover, it can be seen by simply asking people where they have their central plaza. When this is pointed out, the questioner knows exactly where to look for the house of the senior political leader of the settlement since his household is always at the bottom of the U in the center facing west. Parenthetically, this means that when individuals or groups pray and bow down toward the east in the open plaza, which they often do, they face the doorway of their local political leader's compound.

Around the villages are fields of millet, the major food staple, guinea corn, ground-nuts, the major cash crop, and numerous specialized crops of vegetables or gourds that vary from place to place depending upon local conditions. Almost everybody does a little farming while goods not produced within the household itself are purchased at local weekly markets that dot the countryside in each of the major villages.

In their culture the Kanuri share ideas about religion, social organization, and subsistence patterns with many of the other peoples of the Western Sudan. Even esoteric items such as pre-pubescent boys' hair styles are shared across wide areas of the southern and central Sahara ranging as far away as Morocco. In their patterns of dress—workshirts and long ground-length robes for men, long shirts and saris for women—they again share many items with surrounding peoples as they do in their love of horses which give a man prestige unless he is one of the few in the cities that owns an automobile. Their language, Kanuri, is not related to other languages of Nigeria, but is shared and closely related to a large group of tongues called Central Saharan that ranges from the Tibesti highlands in northern Chad to Bornu in the southwest and the Darfur region in the modern nation of Sudan, in the southeast. It is a graceful language in which the verb comes at the end of the sentence as in Latin and in which there are many polite circumlocutions for saying things diplomatically. Thus if I wish to say a man is untrustworthy, I do not say it outright. Instead I say quietly that he has narrow eyes, which comes from the saying, "A man with narrow eyes has no shame," he lacks proper respect for his obligations to others. There are many greetings which are adjusted to social rank,

GATHERING THE MATERIAL · 7

so that one can say "Hello" to a social inferior, to an equal, or to a respected superior, and receive a proper reply recognizing the same distinction. People from other
areas of Nigeria and Europeans claim it is a difficult language to learn. But this
is probably due to the fact that the most widespread language of Northern Nigeria
is Hausa, and many outsiders find they can get along with Hausa in the cities and
larger towns without having to make the effort to learn Kanuri. Certainly today most
Kanuri school children know some Hausa, and facility with it is spreading throughout all of Northern Nigeria.

Distinctive Kanuri cultural features, things which are of unique Kanuri origin, are not necessarily vitally important things. But they are, if you like, diagnostic
features that indicate Bornu-ness in contrast to the cultures of other closely related
ethnic groups in the Sudan. Perhaps the most striking feature is the women's hair
style. At its most resplendent, it resembles the form of a Trojan helmet made out of
an enormous braided ponytail that begins as a crest at the front-center of the head
and curves up over the head to end in a slight upward curl of the tail at the back.
Today a few of the young school girls are beginning to give up this traditional
Kanuri coiffure and are taking on instead the Shuwa-Arab style of a smooth top of
the head with hundreds of small braids clinging tightly to the sides and back of the
head, at the ends of which are either loose ringlets or a pageboy effect.

Other features which are unique to Bornu are their knives and calabash
carvings. These items are also unique to each ethnic group in the region, as are
tribal marks cut on the face. Thus many unique features of Kanuri traditional life
are thought of locally by many peoples as differentiating criteria for separating one
ethnic group from another. A Northern Nigerian going to a market in Jos, or Maiduguri, or Kano, can spot a Kanuri, Fulani, or a Hausa calabash design at a glance
just as he can tell another person's ethnic group by his tribal marks, or spot a
Bornu knife among a pile of others.

On the other hand, the inside of a Kanuri gentleman's household is not
significantly different from the household of a man of similar rank, wealth, occupation, and education, who lives in Hausa country seven or eight hundred miles to
the west of Bornu. They dress in a very similar manner, eat very similar food, and
share many of the same beliefs and attitudes about what is the best way to live,
make decisions, treat one's family, friends, superiors, and worship one's God. Thus
although there are some clear-cut diagnostic features representative of Kanuri culture, the people share in a way of life that is practiced by millions in the Sudan, or
southern savannah land border of the Sahara desert.

Gathering the Material

I first arrived in Bornu in January 1956 and stayed there until August
1957. My next contacts occurred in the summers of 1964 and again in 1965, and
hopefully I shall return in the future to study specialized topics to deepen my understanding of this society as it changes and progresses in the modern world. During our first visit my wife and I spent most of our time in the small village of Magumeri about thirty-three miles northwest of the capital. This was our home base.
From here we also visited other parts of the emirate, especially the larger village of

Geidam in the north, where another anthropologist, Abraham Rosman, and his wife were working. Discussions with Dr. and Mrs. Rosman helped all of us to see many of the unique features of Kanuri life that stemmed from our particular towns as against more general Kanuri patterns of behavior that were widespread throughout the society. We also became acutely aware of the kinds of variations that could occur across communities as they varied in size, ethnic composition, and quality of the political leadership. At the end of the first field trip, my wife and I spent three months in the capital city of Maiduguri looking at government reports and district notebooks, and acquainting ourselves with many of the special activities that characterize courtly life at the center of the emirate.

In 1964 and again in 1965 I returned to Bornu. On my previous visit the country had been a colonial holding of Great Britain, now it was part of the independent nation of Nigeria. My task in this second visit was to gather statistics on marriage and on divorce rates. But it also gave me a chance to see old friends, and catch up on what had been happening locally since my last visit seven years earlier. Some changes were readily apparent. A large number of deep wells were sunk all over the province, and these now provide enough water for a greatly expanded livestock population. Everywhere the cattle are healthier, fatter, and above all much more in evidence. They block roads and are seen herded in large numbers to and fro wherever one wanders over the countryside. Furthermore the people are less afflicted by parasites because the deep water is uncontaminated, as much of it was not during my first visit. There is now a large modern abattoir and a ground-nut oil refinery in the capital city, and in late 1964 the Nigerian railway finally pushed through to Maiduguri to connect the Bornu capital with Nigeria's national railway system. On the other hand, detailed questions about various traditional practices indicated that there have been few changes at the cultural and social level. At the political level where there were English District Officers and other officials of the regional government, now these posts are filled by Nigerians, generally from other parts of northern Nigeria. However it is for the most part correct to use the present tense in describing Bornu, and when this is not true I will attempt to mention the special circumstances that have brought on the changes.

Magumeri, our home for seventeen months in 1956 and 1957, sits on top of one of the ridges of Bornu, and there is a steep climb onto it from the motor road that travels along the bottom of the ridge for most of the year. During the rains, the road runs along the sandy top of the ridge, to keep clear of the large muddy areas formed at the ridge bottom. Magumeri includes approximately 2000 people about half of whom live in surrounding hamlets within the boundaries of the village area. It is a district capital and thus has a two-room primary school, a court house, and the large compound of the district head who administers twenty-one village areas, containing 50,000 people, living in an area of approximately 850 square miles. The village has a weekly market on Sunday, and is divided up into a number of wards under the village area head who is also the political leader of its surrounding hamlets and officially the political subordinate of the district head. Except for the fact that it has a somewhat lower proportion of non-Kanuri compared to most others, Magumeri is a "typical" Bornu village in terms of its size, occupational ranges of the population, and influences it receives from the capital and the world beyond the emirate. Indeed this is why I chose to spend most of my time there. That it did not turn out to be "typical" in all respects is not surprising, given the relatively large numbers of people there are in Bornu and the range of variation that such a large population can quite normally exhibit.

For the first week or so in Magumeri, the Bornu Native Authority appointed a young man who was to serve as our interpreter and guide—telling the people our purpose in coming to live in their village and helping us to get settled into our new surroundings. At first the local Magumeri officials found it all hard to believe, and kept asking why we wanted to live right in the village, rather than reopening an old, deserted, and I suspected snake infested and ramshackle government rest house about a mile away. However, they politely accepted our firm desire to live in the village even if they disagreed with the idea. Soon I decided to live at the end of the plaza facing the district chief's compound, across the open 200 yards of sand which stretched between his house and mine. The interpreter helped with all these arrangements, and in the ten days he was with us I took down a rough outline of the entire culture using him as an informant. As an interpreter, he accompanied me to the compound of the village area head and we asked if I could take down his genealogy and that of some of his neighbors in order that people might become acquainted with the kinds of questions I would be asking later on. At the same time, my wife began compiling a short dictionary of Kanuri nouns, verbs, and useful phrases, using our interpreter as her major source.

For the next four months, we struggled to learn the language and to get our house built—it kept falling down all the time we lived in it—and to begin making a few friends. The first ten days had been so rich and fruitful that what came afterwards seemed all the harder to accept. Without the language, very little could be accomplished; we could watch but not ask questions about what it all meant. The local school teacher who knew very little English offered his help. He would teach us Kanuri, he said, help us to understand the customs of the people, if we would help him to learn English. And slowly this exchange blossomed into a close friendship that has lasted through the years. Slowly, too, little phrases of Kanuri conversation jumped out at us as understandable items from a background of unintelligible conversation. In about four months my wife and I could converse haltingly with one another, and in six months we were speaking—with an accent, with bad grammar, and a limited vocabulary—but we were speaking nonetheless.

During this first six months, several significant things happened that affected the course of our work. First, the district head who mistrusted us when we had arrived began to relax when nothing dire seemed to follow from our presence on his doorstep. Eventually he and I became friends and his acceptance of our presence in Bornu, and Magumeri in particular, along with his conviction that I was in fact studying the customs of his people, helped and many others followed his lead. Secondly, I became very ill with hepatitis, and had to leave Magumeri for two months. No one (we were told later) believed for a minute that we would ever return after such a dreadful illness—but we did. And our return was a triumphant one. For several days visitors poured in to tell us what had been happening during my illness, and what was going to happen, and so on. We had come home, we said, and Magumeri made us feel that it was indeed a homecoming.

Slowly but surely life settled into a pattern and my wife and I became identifiable members of the community and known throughout the entire emirate as "the Europeans of Magumeri." This pattern involved interviewing and visiting households in Magumeri and its surrounding hamlets during the morning, asking questions about household life, farming, and the social relations within the household and between its members and the wider community. Along with attendance at ceremonies, these morning activities came to be defined locally as my "work." My wife, not a trained anthropologist, visited a number of her women friends in the mornings, and looked after household matters. However, she was a part of Magumeri women's society, and we gained insights from her friendships that would have been difficult for a man to achieve by himself. In the afternoon we very often visited with a group of the young men who were associates of the school teacher. They became our intimate friends, and were defined locally as such. During these sessions, we participated in the conversation, or listened, often breaking in to ask questions about the meaning of some event being discussed. Sometimes data collected elsewhere in the mornings, would be discussed with our friends—hiding the identity of the informant when possible—in order to more fully understand what it was that had been collected.

This rather regular schedule was punctuated with visits to see the district head, visits to other villages, and a trip into Maiduguri, the capital, every month for a day or two to obtain supplies for the household. Special events such as the visit of another chief, or a touring British official, also broke the regularity of our days. But in general time stopped. We were without newspapers, radio, television, and even our mail was collected only when we went in once a month to the city. In this way, news from the world outside Bornu reached us first through Kanuri perspectives. Thus when the Suez crisis began in 1957 we heard of it from a young cattle inoculator who was living in Magumeri and had brought a battery radio with him. He told us and a large crowd that the British had attacked and "were killing the Muslims," but that the Russians and the Chinese were supporting the Muslims and were going to kill all the British. For days we were asked the relative population figures of Great Britain, Russia, and China, and really did not get the story straight ourselves for a day or so.

Later, after more than ten months of fieldwork, I began thinking of gathering some questionnaire data on farming, marketing, status rating of occupations, and family budgets. The latter was attached to morning visits and became a part of the work in each household. A field assistant already trained in gathering statistical data on crops asked a set of questions of seventy-five farmers in three villages, including Magumeri, where he was carrying on a fertilizer demonstration. Later this same young man did some work collecting information on kinship behavior among a number of people throughout Bornu. Much later still, after we moved to the capital, we asked school officials there to allow us to question the Maiduguri school children which we did *en masse* using the help of school teachers and Dr. and Mrs. Rosman. All the pupils were asked questions about the status rating of occupations, and about their marriage preferences with particular ethnic groups. These questionnaire data were extremely useful since they could be utilized to check some major conclusions concerning a whole series of attitudes, as well as economic and kinship behavior which involved a great deal of variation across the population. However it is important to note that such highly selective data collection had to be done at the end of the field trip when we knew what questions to ask and could interpret answers in light of our broader understanding of the cultural context.

In summary, then, the methods were those traditionally associated with social anthropology, namely a long period in the field, learning the language, getting to know the people on a face to face basis, while participating, observing, and asking questions about the local social life. This is the basic experience from which the material described in this book is drawn.

Ethnography and Theory

By definition a case study such as this involves a description of the way of life of a people. However, no description is ever complete, nor is it a sheer listing of facts. The facts are related to one another, and many are left out. The basis for selection is, whether he knows it or not, a net result of the writer's theories and his biases. In this present work I have decided to describe what I consider to be the most important aspect of Kanuri society, and by this I mean those features which are its most determinant or causal aspects. This kind of approach can be seen more clearly when put into the form of a question phrased as follows: What are the set of organized activities by which the Kanuri of Bornu have adapted to their environment, and created means for the maintenance, continuity, and evolution of their society? Specifically, I have tried to answer this question by showing how each of the major sectors of Kanuri social life, the family, the household, the individual life experience, the political, and the economic systems, are related to one another, through their use of the household organization and its modes of behavior. The household is a model, and a building block as well, upon which the rest of the complicated activities of the Bornu society rests. I will come back to this point in the concluding chapter after having described the way in which the society actually works as a "system," or an organized whole, in accordance with this theory. However it should be noted that I have excluded religion and ceremonial life as "major sectors." For purposes of this report I consider them superfluous to the problem outlined above and have therefore mentioned them only when such material seems necessary. Even then they are integrated into other sectors and not treated separately.

It is up to the reader to ask whether or not I have made a convincing case by using this theory, or whether these facts could be explained in ways other than the manner they are interpreted here. If skepticism holds firm, the reader should ask whether my interpretation would be weakened if facts not presented here were described. He should also ask himself what these facts might be, and how he would go about collecting them. Ethnography is in one sense a naïve undertaking, especially for a society as complicated and ancient as that of the Kanuri. How can we ever say we have adequately described a whole society of nearly one million people whose traditions go back a thousand years? Obviously we can't. And so we attempt instead to capture its essence. In what is to follow I have tried to do just that. If I am wrong, or naïve, or illogical, I am also of the anthropological faith which preaches that the attempt to understand a human society through fieldwork is a scientifically useful one besides being one of the most profound experiences that life has to offer.

2

History

Kanem-Bornu: The Historical Background

THIS BOOK is primarily an account of the way of life of a contemporary African people. However this particular group, unlike many others in Africa or elsewhere, has an ancient and well-documented history. The fact that such materials are available also means that we can observe the kingdom as it developed through time and obtain some appreciation for its continuity and change as one of the oldest political powers in Africa. I have therefore tried to bring together in summary form an account of Bornu history and its political development during the last millenium of southern Saharan history. In terms of the overall ethnographic task it is important to realize that it is within this historical stream that the contemporary way of life has come to be what it is. Indeed one of the most salient facts about Kanuri culture is the pride the people feel in their history; they believe that one cannot know them unless there is at the same time some understanding of their past. In order to do this I have written first an outline of the major events of this history, then analyzed the political development of the kingdom as it evolved through time. The details of the present political system are then taken up again in Chapter 6.

Kanuri legends all take the Bornu kingdom back to the north and northeast of Lake Chad to the ancient kingdom of Kanem and before that to Yemen. Like many peoples of West Africa as far removed from one another as the Yoruba of Nigeria and the Fulani of Futa Djallon in Guinea, Kanuri traditions suggest that they as a people come originally from Yemen. It is said that a migrant Yemenite noble named Sef founded the royal dynasty of the Magumi Sefuwa. There is very little doubt that the ancient dynasty of the Sefuwa has been in fact the ruling line in Kanem-Bornu for over a thousand years. However, there is very little evidence except for the legend itself to support the theory that the Kanuri or their ancient leaders originate in Yemen.

The problem of studying human origins scientifically is a fascinating one, but there are many pitfalls and a keen taste for skepticism is a primary requirement. The rules of the game are, however, quite easy. Simply ask what valid facts are available, then try for the best explanation knowing that new facts will very probably force a change in the historical picture you have created to best explain the facts. The greater the number of facts, the fewer the possible number of different historical interpretations that can be applied to any particular case. With these rules in mind let us examine briefly what facts are at hand to help us with Kanuri origins.

First of all we have the Kanuri legends themselves which state that they came originally from Yemen—a legend they share with most of the Muslim people of the western Sudan. Let us call this the local theory and come back to it after considering other available facts. Subsistence farming and cattle keeping came into the area of the central and western Sahara about 5000 years ago, as evidenced by a number of archaeological sites in the area. At that time the Tibesti region north of Lake Chad was much wetter and the lake itself was enormous. It stretched well into the Sahara desert, especially into a region just south of the Tibesti known as the Bodele depression, which even today is well below the present level of Lake Chad itself. People settled in this region and utilized both domesticated plants and animals for their basic means of subsistence. Since that time, however, there has been a steady desiccation of the central Sahara which has dried up the Tibesti and the Bodele depression while the water has retreated in a southwesterly direction towards the present site of Lake Chad. As late as 500 B.C. merchants from Carthage were voyaging to the Tibesti to trade with people who lived in a wet climate among crocodiles, hippopotami, and giraffes.[1] Certainly what evidence we have suggests a very ancient trade between the people of the entire Sahara and those of North Africa. This was much expanded by the introduction of the camel sometime in the first or second century A.D. which facilitated trade across much drier portions of desert and over much longer distances. If we add to this evidence the fact that the Kanuri language is related to the central Saharan group of languages—and these are as a group only very distantly related to all other African language families—then a picture or at least a theory begins to emerge.

The Neolithic agriculturalists in the southern Sahara were drawn further south between 1000 B.C. and 1000 A.D. as the waters of the desert began to recede southward.[2] As they moved southward they pulled the Saharan trade with them, and competition among groups in the Chad basin produced some differences in power and recognized status among clans who lived in the area. Leading lineages within these clans began to unite to govern the activities of clan members until finally the various clans formed loose federations with a leading clan and its leading lineage as the royal or kingly one.[3]

---

[1] See Rhys Carpenter, "A Trans-Saharan Caravan Route in Herodotus," *Journal of American Archaeology*, Vol. 60, 1956, pp. 231–42.

[2] This process was also occurring in another area of "desert capture," the upper Niger bend where desert wet regions north of the river receded towards the south. The Niger itself bends into the Sahara, because like the Chad basin there are lowlands to the north of the great bend. Thus it is no accident that the Chad basin and the upper Niger bend have witnessed some of the earliest developments of centralized states in the western Sudan—they were the two areas into which the people of the desert could most naturally and easily move as desiccation proceeded.

[3] In his book on Bunyoro, John Beattie very concisely defines a lineage as "all the descendants in one line (that is, either through males only or through females only) of a particular person through a specified number of generations. It differs from a *clan* in that while usually all the

Given the fact that very many of the Muslim peoples of West Africa have legends concerning their origins in the Near East and often more specifically in Yemen, we can, I believe, think of the local origin theory as a mythical genesis story that is part of a widespread cultural heritage of the Muslim people of West Africa, likening it in this way to western stories about the Garden of Eden. On the other hand we do have "hard" linguistic evidence that the Kanuri people are related to peoples of the central Sahara northeast of Bornu. We also have very suggestive evidence from the geographic history that relates the people speaking these languages to one another and gives us grounds for positing immigration into the Chad basin and an increasing population density in the area. The exact details of this theory are matters for future research, but the major conclusion which places the origin of the Kanuri in the central Sahara seems to be a valid one.

At any rate, by the end of the first millennium A.D. the Muslim world outside the Sudan knew of the existence of Kanem, a sovereign state due south of Tripoli on the southern rim of the Sahara. Local traditions associated with the king lists (these have been collected periodically since 1850) assert that Islam came at least to the rulers of Kanem in the eleventh century. According to the traditions an eleventh-century Mai or king is supposed to have died in Egypt on his way to Mecca. Certainly by the twelfth and thirteenth centuries Kanem became a well-known state in the Islamic world. Trans-Saharan commerce was completely controlled, garrisons were built to protect the trade routes, and treaty relations were established with the Hafsid rulers of Tunis. In the mid-thirteenth century a travelers' house for Kanem pilgrims was constructed in Cairo so that they might have proper accommodation while on the long journey to Mecca via Egypt. At the other extreme of the Islamic world, in Spain, a poet from Kanem was renowned in the court of El Mansur (1190–1214 A.D.) in Seville for his praise songs of the Sultan. This was a great period of Islamic civilization and Kanem played its part in that florescence.

From the mid-thirteenth to the end of the fourteenth century a period of dark ages befell the kingdom. This is sometimes referred to as "the time of troubles." The dynastic chronicles indicate this period by including a great many rulers all holding sway for very short periods. The kingdom seems to have become a tempestuous stage for civil wars within and continuous attack from without. A letter to Cairo from this period has turned up, sent by a Kanem ruler, asking that the Caliph of Egypt send word to Sudanese Arabs who were helping Wadai to the east of Kanem raid amongst the people of Kanem for slaves even though such actions are considered to be against the precepts of Islam, since one must not raid for slaves amongst other Muslim peoples.[4] The main source of trouble is supposed to have come from one particular group—the Bulala. These people were either an allied subordinate tribe or a clan whose leading lineage had split off from the Kanem royal line and had then grown in its independence and power until its leaders challenged the Kanem control of the kingdom.

members of a lineage know exactly how they are related to all the other members of it, and together, they often form a corporate group, clan members may not be able to trace genealogical links with other clan members, and often clansfolk are widely dispersed." See John Beattie, *Bunyoro: An African Kingdom,* Case Studies in Cultural Anthropology, (New York: Holt, Rinehart and Winston, Inc., 1960), p. 3.

[4] See R. H. Palmer, *Bornu, Sahara, and Sudan,* (London: John Murray, 1936), p. 195.

Finally in the late fourteenth century, a rebellious Bulala group east of Lake Chad upset the Magumi Sefuwa rulers of Kanem, who ultimately came to the south-west portion of the Chad basin to establish what later became the empire of Bornu.

The collapse of the great Kanem empire in the fourteenth century is attributed by tradition to internal civil wars resulting from the Bulala revolt against the Sefuwa dynasty. The ultimate cause is rationalized in legend by an alleged irreligious act of the seventeenth king or Mai of Kanem, one Dunama, (ca. 1220–1260 A.D.) who is supposed to have "laid the foundations for the ensuing disaster of the empire by opening the sacred talisman of Bornu" which subsequently provoked men of ambition to entreat against the state.[5] It may or may not be true, but it is very likely not the entire explanation even if we were to know what the "sacred talisman" was—which we do not; knowledge of its meaning and content have long since disappeared. Other reasons for the collapse of the kingdom besides that of a civil war against the Bulala can be suggested. The kingdom was in all likelihood not highly centralized and the nobles could quite easily unite, obtain outside help, and try to gain control. Indeed all of the traditions of the Bulala tell of them obtaining help from the Tubu of the central Sahara (a rebellious group who were tributary to Kanem) against the ruling Kanem dynasty.

Another factor is the nature of succession to the throne. Throughout the Sudan, and for as long as any traditions go back in Bornu, succession to the throne has always been open to those whose fathers have been monarchs. However, given many short reigns, this custom increases the number of contenders enormously and therefore exacerbates competition for royal office in the state so that the danger of civil wars and lack of unity is accelerated; the state is then much weakened as an effective political force. In other words, given a few short reigns, the possibility that more will follow becomes even greater unless a strong man with very strong backing emerges to quell the factions supporting various royal contenders. Finally it should be realized that Bornu was a much greener land than Kanem and it might have actually attracted the Kanem ruling group and their followers away from the drier, more inhospitable northern shores of Lake Chad. Certainly the kingdom of Kanem was not of such a nature that it suddenly collapsed when people (later to be called Kanuri) left. The Bulala clan assumed the leadership and Kanem continued as a sovereign state while the Kanuri tried, unsuccessfully at first, to reconquer their lost empire.

By the end of the fifteenth century the Sefuwa and their clan, the Magumi, had obtained sovereignty to the southwest of Lake Chad, and under a series of able monarchs they established their new kingdom of Bornu as a great power in the Sudan. The first of these rulers to organize and establish a really powerful state was a man named Ali Ghajedeni (ca. 1470–1500 A.D.), the forty-eighth monarch on the Sefuwa dynastic list. He built a new capital called Birni Ngazargamo, "the walled fortress," at the north end of Bornu and united this new kingdom under his control. Ali is supposed to have reconquered Kanem and re-established control over the Saharan trade while making war continually against Songhai to the west over the subjugation of the Hausa states and the east-west trade routes across the Sudan. His reign was followed by a series of others no less nota-

[5] H. Barth, *Travels and Discoveries in North and Central Africa*, Vol. II, (London: Longmans, Green & Co., Ltd., 1857), p. 637.

ble, and these men maintained Bornu at an apogee of greatness until well into the seventeenth century. One of these rulers, Idris Alooma, had a court scribe at the beginning of the seventeenth century, who wrote a number of accounts of his royal master's military expeditions. Luckily these have survived to give us a picture of Bornu warfare and government in the late sixteenth and early seventeenth centuries. It was during this period, too, that Bornu was first mentioned on European maps, and from this time forward its fame became part of the legends of unknown kingdoms that lay inside the unexplored interior of Africa.

Bornu traditions claim that the seventeenth and eighteenth centuries witnessed a decline in the power of the state. This is explained by the claim that the monarchy was becoming weak and overburdened with pomp, rituals, and religious study by the monarch. The ruling Mai appeared in public in a *fanadir,* or cage, which only his most trusted servants could approach and rarely led military expeditions himself. Much of this may be a reinterpretation of Bornu history by the second dynasty and their followers, who would naturally have played up the failures of the previous regime, when they took over in the nineteenth century. Contrarily there are traditions of many successful military campaigns during this period and Bornu's reputation as a great kingdom was still very widespread. Thus a wandering Englishman, Richard Tulley, who visited Tripoli at the end of the eighteenth century, spoke glowingly of what he had heard of Bornu's power. Parenthetically, he claimed that one of the Kanuri noblewomen living in Tripoli could speak the Italian language fluently.[6] On the other side of the case, Tuareg and Tubu raiders attacked the northern boundaries of Bornu and harassed the caravans with greater intensity than before.

The activities of these raiders are said to have increased during the seventeenth and eighteenth centuries, but it is important to realize that the entire southern Sahara was a hotbed of unrest during this two hundred year period. In the 1590s the armies of El Mansur of Morocco finally managed to cross the Sahara and destroy the great empire of Songhai. Its cities of Timbuctu and Gau never again became the great emporia of trade, politics, and learning they had once been. The Moroccans could not establish, so far from home, any stable administrative organization capable of replacing the one they had destroyed. This suddenly released vassal groups in the Sahara, many of whom bordered on Bornu, and these were now free to raid, stimulate revolts, and pillage caravans, while their cousins to the west fought over the remains of the Songhai empire and the control of western trade routes across the Sahara. It was during this same period of unrest that, all across the Sudan, wandering holy men, especially nomadic Fulani of Futa Djallon in Guinea, in Masina in the Upper Niger, and even in present day Nigeria, were expressing this disorder in religious terms. They preached through their leaders for a return to a truer and purer form of Islam. Often they claimed that those round them were pagans and had to be subdued in a holy war to reestablish Muslim order and law. It is in the light of all this turbulence that the so-called decline of Bornu in the seventeenth and eighteenth centuries should be seen. Elsewhere empires were tottered or being formed, as in Futa Djallon; but Bornu remained, shaken perhaps by the general unrest of the period but still it survived, controlled its trade routes,

---

[6] R. Tulley, *Letters Written During a Ten Years' Residence at the Court of Tripoli,* Vol. II, (London: 1819), p. 51.

ruled its territory, and attempted to keep the peace with its neighbors and tributary states.

At the beginning of the nineteenth century, the area of what is now Northern Nigeria was rocked by the Fulani wars under a religious leader, Othman dan Fodio, who proclaimed a *Jihad* or holy war. Ultimately these developments resulted in the founding of the empire of Sokoto. In Bornu the local Fulani organized an attack on the Kanuri kingdom, not so much to support the Sokoto Empire, as to take advantage of it and set up principalities of their own. By 1808, the Fulani in Bornu constituted a dangerous threat. Indeed they had succeeded in attacking, defeating and sacking the ancient capital of Bornu, Birni Ngazargamo. When this happened the ruler and his followers fled towards Lake Chad and were not able to return to the city until some unexpected aid from Kanem enabled them to deliver a powerful defeat to the Fulani forces some six weeks after they had abandoned the capital. A few years later in the winter of 1811–1812 another Fulani force attacked and pillaged the capital. Again the Kanuri were helped by this same Kanembu chief or Shehu who defeated the Fulani and sent them fleeing westward to the borders of Bornu.

However, this aid was to change the entire history of the empire. From 1812 onwards the traditional Bornu government lost its control of the state. The Shehu, Mohammed el Aminu, El Kanemi, or Shehu Laminu as he is remembered locally, had the only effective armed force in the Bornu kingdom, and he used this to control sporadic Fulani uprisings that continued until at least the 1820s. Both the traditional government and the Shehu moved away from the western and northern boundaries and set up in adjacent towns near the west shore of Lake Chad. People soon realized that the Shehu held power in the state and flocked to his town, while that of the old Magumi Sefuwa monarch became a small redoubt for those still loyal to the ancient dynasty. The former leaders still retained the royal title, held court, and collected or were given some of the state revenues. When they intrigued against Shehu Laminu, he simply deposed them. At the same time he made bargains with rival claimants to the old throne so that any changes in the royal office, made under his direction, would be to his own advantage. Meanwhile the ancient rulers came more and more to be simply ceremonial puppets in the hands of the real ruler of Bornu, Shehu Laminu.

Yet Laminu never asserted ultimate control over the kingdom. Even after he had built a new capital, at Kuka, for himself and his dependents, the small village of Birni nearby was maintained for the ancient monarchy. Across the entire Sudan and beyond, however, he was recognized as the real ruler of Bornu. He was the leader of its administration and his political, military, and judicial sagacity were and still are lauded in praise songs that match these secular skills with his supernatural powers. Indeed his fame spread to Europe as well. This resulted from the writings of Denham and Clapperton, who crossed the desert in the 1820s and remained for an extended period in Bornu learning about its people and of the double regency under Shehu Laminu's control. Laminu died in 1835 and it was not until a decade later in 1845 or 1846 that his son, Omar, finally did away with the last remaining members of the Sefuwa dynasty proclaiming himself and his royal heirs to be the only rulers of Bornu. This was the occasion for the formal inception of Bornu's second dynasty whose descendants are the ruling family in the kingdom at the present time. It was during Shehu Omar's reign that Barth, the famous African explorer, visited Bornu and obtained the first written account of its history.

The descendants of Shehu Laminu ruled throughout the rest of the nineteenth century without undue excitement. There were always succession problems indicated by struggles for the throne among possible heirs and during the 1850s there was even a revolt in which a prince of the realm overturned his older brother for a few months until the deposed monarch was able to gather his forces and recapture the government. But such events had always been the common currency of Bornu's history.

Later in the century, however, a tragedy befell the kingdom. A marauding brigand of the Sudan who had gathered around himself an army of well-disciplined and trained soldiers slashed his way westward across Africa conquering and pillaging as he went. In 1893 he crossed over into Bornu and demolished the capital, defeating the Bornu army and sending the Shehu with some of his followers fleeing to the north and west of Bornu. This man, Rabeh, is still remembered today in Bornu for the tyrannical hold he attempted to establish and for the plundering and sacking of many Bornu villages which he carried out while subduing the state. Eventually he built himself a capital in southeast Bornu and married his daughter to the son of the Emir of Sokoto. Rabeh provides some interesting grounds for speculation. For had colonial expansion into the area not conflicted with Rabeh's own plans, he might very likely have founded Bornu's third dynasty. As it was Britain, France, and Germany were carving up West Africa for themselves.

The French arrived first and soon found themselves at war with Rabeh. Eventually he was defeated and killed, and although his sons attempted to keep control of their father's new found kingdom, it was a futile gesture in the face of French arms. By 1902 the British had taken over what is now Bornu province in northeastern Nigeria; the Germans obtained the Cameroons—containing Rabeh's old capital, and the French set up their headquarters at Fort Lamy in what is now Chad. The old Kanembu Shehu was put on the throne again by the French at Dikwa (Rabeh's capital) and was then maintained by the Germans. In the scramble over territory that characterized this period, the British persuaded the Shehu to return to Nigerian territory, where they have been ever since as rulers of Bornu.

The British first brought the Shehu to Kuka, the nineteenth-century capital of the Kanembu Shehus, which they had promised to rebuild for him as part of the bargain for his return. They set up their own headquarters in the village of Magumeri and tried to administer the state from these two centers. The job of administration from Magumeri proved impossible, as did the prospect of rebuilding Kuka; it had been sacked and demolished during the Rabeh period. In 1905 the colonial government decided to set up a new capital at Maiduguri in southern Bornu which would serve as a center for both the emirate and the Province of Bornu. Today it still serves both these functions and is the major urban center of the area.

The British also reorganized the political structure of the state, and geared it into the wider colonial government they were evolving for Northern Nigeria as a whole under the leadership of Lord Lugard. Under Lugard's direction they also stopped the trans-Saharan trade, especially in slaves, and oriented Bornu's economy southwards towards the Guinea Coast and the rest of Nigeria. In 1914 they quietly, and with practically no incident, took over the Northern Cameroons from the Germans and ruled it after World War I as a League of Nations Trust Territory, (later a U.N. Trust Territory) which meant in practice that it was part of the administrative responsibility of the colonial officials in Northern Nigeria. To appreciate more clearly what changes were brought about by colonialism, however, it is necessary to understand something of the social, economic, and in particular the political structure of Bornu, as it developed during pre-colonial times, and it is to this task that the remainder of the chapter is devoted.

Kanem-Bornu: The Social and Political Background

Only the sketchiest oddments of information are available about the nature of Kanem society. One Arabic record speaks of its capital as a city of tents, and traditions tell of a "Council of Nobles" that had a great deal of power over decision-making by the king, or Mai as he was called. From this and a few other data, such as the emphasis placed on the clan membership of persons mentioned in the early periods of the dynastic lists, we can attempt a reconstruction that fits the facts. The early kingdom seems to have been made up of patrilineal, named clans under senior or noble lineages (also named) whose heads formed the so-called "Council of Nobles" under the king or Mai. The Mai himself was head of the senior lineage of a senior clan considered to be the most important or powerful in the region. In all probability the term "Mai" or "king" was used for all leaders of clans just as it is today among some of the nomadic and semi-nomadic peoples of the Sahara to the north of Lake Chad who are closely related to the Kanuri. It also appears that the great Kanuri king lists are just what local people say they are—lists of the leaders of the Magumi Sefuwa or Sefuwa lineage heads of the Magumi clan. People in the clan considered themselves related by ties of descent to a common ancestor; but they could not describe the exact link with him, while they could describe the genealogical ties through men that made them all Sefuwa. Very probably these people utilized both cattle and domesticated plants although their early city of tents, referred to by Arabic historians, also suggests a greater emphasis on nomadism and the use of cattle. This is consistent with the clan organization described above; indeed this form of organization is widespread among nomadic and semi-nomadic peoples in the Sahara, North Africa, the Horn of Africa, and Arabia. Later, as attested by the ruins at Garamoulé northwest of Lake Chad they probably built more permanent settlements and very likely used slaves from the south of Lake Chad as trade goods and as agricultural laborers.

How centralized and developed the early stages of the Kanem state really were is an intriguing and difficult question and one that can be solved only by extensive historical and archaeological research. Certainly concepts of statecraft from Islamic areas to the north of the desert and trips by Kanem monarchs to Mecca would have acquainted the rulers with the ideas of very highly centralized states. How much this actually affected Bornu is unknown, although it is possible that tensions over the power of the central monarch were another reason for the civil strife which led eventually to the migration of the Sefuwa from Kanem to Bornu.

After the Sefuwa set up their kingdom in Bornu the state became a much more highly organized and centrally controlled political system. The people who came to Bornu—and who also came to be called Kanuri about this time—were the Sefuwa, their fellow Magumi clansmen and loyal followers, clients and slaves. The traditions declare that the leader who finally founded the new capital of Birni Ngazargamo curbed the power of his own nobles and insisted that all of them (except one who protected the western boundaries) should live in the capital, leaving subordinates to administer their fief-holdings.[7] It should also be remembered that this newly formed Bornu kingdom (*ca.* 1450–1550 A.D.) tried to regain control over Kanem and many of its other lost vassal territories in the Chad Basin and the southern desert. Thus they very quickly attacked and defeated Bilma 400 miles to the north of Lake Chad which was the center for the Saharan salt trade. They also had to defend the kingdom against raiding desert Tuareg and the rising power of Songhai in the west.

Kanem was a state organized around a confederacy of clans, with one clan and its leading lineage having a senior status. The migration of this leading group into Bornu helps to explain why the Bornu kingdom was more centralized than its predecessor as a political system. In Bornu the Magumi Sefuwa had no other related clan or clan leaders to share power with; instead they were confronted by a group of pagan peoples spoken of under the general term of "So" in the traditions. Against these people they fought battles of conquest to establish their rule in the area and in the end absorbed many of them into a group known today as the Kanuri. It would have been much simpler to unify this one group under a leader who had no rival clan or clan leaders to cope with. Thus the new situation in Bornu afforded both a stimulus and an opportunity for increased centralization of power in the political organization of the Kanuri state. It is against this growing centralization in the hands of the ruling monarch of Bornu that the following account of its structure should be gauged, for it is not always easy to portray change and development while describing how a society is organized.

Pre-nineteenth Century Bornu

At the head of the early Bornu state was the Mai or king. This office was hereditary in the male line, and all men whose fathers had been monarchs were eligible for the succession. The Council of Nobles, and accounts vary as to who these were, chose the new monarch upon the death of the reigning one, although powerful rulers could obviously affect the choice. The royal office carried with it an aura of untouchability, remoteness, and sacredness. People referred to the Mai as "Master" using the term applied by slaves to their owners. People approached the royal cage in which the Mai was seated and prostrated themselves before the bars putting sand on their heads or going through the motions of doing so to indicate the humility and respect they felt in his presence.

Members of the royal family held titled offices. These included the monarch's own mother, his senior wife, and often a senior female relative, either a sister, half-sister, or more distant female relatives in the male line. The sons and

[7] A fief is a political unit within a state over which a superior has rights of tribute collection and political leadership (not necessarily exclusive rights) given to him by his or his ancestors' relationship to a monarch.

daughters of sovereigns were the princes and princesses of the realm. Princesses were often given in marriage by the king to create alliances between the throne and other states, or nobles, or as rewards to trusted followers. Often, one among the princes was designated Chiroma or heir apparent. However, there was no hard and fast rule that the Chiroma either had the title for life, or that having been graced by the title its holder automatically succeeded to the throne. Although there was no special term for royal granddaughter, a king's grandsons who might become princes, if their fathers obtained the throne, were referred to by a special term.

Attached to the royal household by bonds of strict loyalty and obedience were the king's followers, some of whom lived in the palace, while others lived nearby. These, known as Koguna, together with members of the royal family and their followers provided the basis for the nobility of the state. They were of two main types—slave and free—with slaves being divided into ordinary slaves and eunuchs. The slaves originated from the slave trade or from raids made among pagan groups, or from the sons and daughters of slaves. The free nobility came from deroyalized segments of the royal family as it expanded through time and from descendants of nobles. This nobility was the source of personnel for the bulk of the administrative activities of the state. They served as the monarch's personal bodyguard, as messengers, military commanders, tax collectors, trusted spies, praise singers, slave raiders, consuls, and foreign emissaries. From their ranks came the people who bore the major titles of the state. Some of the titles were derived from Islam; others came from earlier times in Kanem or Bornu history. Although much changed in their nature, a number of these have survived to the present day.

In order to administer the kingdom, titled nobles, including the titled women of the royal family, were given fiefs equivalent to what are today village area units. All such holdings were fragmented and dispersed so that no one noble had control over any large portion of the state. The fief holdings varied in size and number per noble and were a measure of the political success of that particular noble at any point in time. The one exception was the Galidima. The holder of this title maintained a large consolidated set of village areas on the western boundary to protect the east-west trade and guard the western approaches to the capital city. The fief-holders raised militia for the monarch and taxes for themselves and the monarch. They also served as an appeal court system for the local people when they wished adjudication at higher than the local level. Thus people could obtain a royal audience by going through the fief hierarchy. The Kanuri also used the widespread Sudanese practice of dividing the kingdom into quadrants based on the four cardinal directions. Over each quadrant was a highly trusted follower of the king who could oversee the administration of his own quadrant, raise direct royal tax levies, and serve as an alternative form of hierarchy between the people and their ruler. The system functioned in this way as a check on the power of fief-holders, since the king could take fiefs away and redistribute them if there was sufficient reason for doing so. Through their own subordinates these quadrant leaders also administered the nomadic peoples of the kingdom who could not be easily worked into the administration of the fief system based as it was on settled populations. Two of the four leaders were always eunuchs, making for an automatically free power of appointment by the monarch, since these men had no heirs. The other two were always chosen from among the king's closest associates, although there was also a tendency for these two titles to be passed on down the male line. Even in this latter case, however, the king could always choose those most likely to be totally loyal to his administration from among the heirs, or even disregard the hereditary rule if he wished and give the title to some other person. The four quadrant leaders also had their own fiefs which they used as the basic support for their large household organizations in the capital.

Vassal groups and territories paid tribute in kind through their leaders to the treasury of the Mai of Bornu. In the heyday of Bornu during the fifteenth and sixteenth centuries these vassals included a large number of surrounding peoples in what is now Northern Nigeria, Niger, and Chad. These subordinate groups were organized in two ways. In the first instance a Bornu consul was appointed to reside in the tributary state to help collect annual tributes and administer the government. This was in effect a kind of conquest and occupation used most often in adjacent and nearby territories. The second method was to leave the territory under the control of its own leaders after they had pledged their loyalty and their intention to pay tributes and give military support to Bornu whenever necessary; they were also expected to provide safety and hospitality to expeditions and caravans going to and from Bornu. Some of these vassal states were caught between two great powers. Such a case were the Hausa of northwestern Nigeria. Caught as they were between Songhai to the west and Bornu to the east they, therefore, paid tributes in two directions, always hoping that someday they could be relieved of these burdens by an increase in their own power or a decrease in the power of one or both of their overlords. Indeed Bornu traditions and written records are almost totally concerned with expeditions against reluctant tributaries who were remiss in the payment of their tributes. On the other hand, there are also accounts of tributary states sending to Bornu for help against external enemies and internal revolts; so the relationship could, and often did, work to the advantage of both the conqueror and the conquered.

The religious and legal life of the state was strongly influenced by the specialized religious practitioners who were steeped in the Koran and Islamic jurisprudence. The chief judge and religious leader of early Bornu was given the title of Talba and is referred to in traditions as "second to the king," or the next in authority to the monarch himself. He and his descendants and client followers knew the Arabic script and thus made up a literate group closely associated with political leaders as scribes, legal advisers and religious functionaries. These men sat in on judicial hearings and advised political leaders who adjudicated on the basis of their own knowledge of the law. Besides the Mai, most noble households kept such religious men within their compounds for similar purposes, and as instructors for the children. Under such conditions the religious leaders were also strong supporters of the state and its power structure.

Little is known of the details of taxation for the early Bornu kingdom although records are much better for the nineteenth century system. Obviously some form of tax was levied on local fiefs by fief-holders as well as by the monarch who also received tributes from vassal states and a major portion of booty from warfare. As we have already noted, it is fairly evident that royal taxation of the Bornu population itself was carried on through the efforts of the monarch's titled followers who held powers of royal taxation privilege in the four quadrants of the state.

Tributes could be quite large; there are records of payments from Kanem to Bornu in the sixteenth century that mention amounts of 1000 head of cattle per year.

Along with taxation and other demands such as annual military service, there was a system of exemption whereby persons or groups were released from their obligations to the state in return for some service—usually prayers and other religious duties. These exemptions, *Mahram,* were made by royal declaration in writing which stipulated that facets of a person's obligation were henceforward considered to be *haram* or forbidden, like the eating of pork. One of the oldest of these, given to the family of Umme Jilma, declares that the family is forever exempt from (a) entertaining the king's men during the dry-season military and tax collection campaigns, (b) from *diya* or blood compensation for injuries inflicted on others by accident, and (c) all forms of tribute and taxes. In time, however, all these exemptions were often honored more in the breach or renegotiated. Thus one sixteenth-century monarch ordered a large group to go to war. These people promptly refused on the basis of a *Mahram* given them by a previous ruler. When the king insisted, the entire group prepared to leave his kingdom. However a compromise was worked out in which they accepted military service and paid practically no taxes. This very same group is mentioned again in the traditions at the beginning of the nineteenth century when Shehu Laminu ruled that their exemptions should pertain only to the leaders of the group, not the entire set of male line descendants of the original holders of this privilege, who by this time had become a very large population.

In its apogee during the fifteenth and sixteenth centuries, the Bornu kingdom was an expansionist power, and warfare was the state function par excellence. According to traditions and written records, as many as seven or eight military campaigns a year were not uncommon; this meant an expedition might leave Bornu every six or eight weeks during the dry season. With so much militarism the techniques of warfare elaborated accordingly. From at least the sixteenth century onward, Bornu imported muskets, swords, chain mail which were vital and ancient parts of the Saharan trade, although such armaments were also manufactured by Bornu craftsmen as well.

The army itself was organized into regiments, representing a local area or an ethnic group under their own leaders, and they went into battle according to a well laid out military strategy. Campaigns were amost always conducted against walled towns. The shield bearers advanced first; then after it was felt that the poison arrows of the enemy were exhausted, the rest of the army would advance either storming the walls or forcing the town dwellers to come out and fight—whereupon muskets and cavalry were used. Generally speaking open encounters were quite unusual; the Bornu army was large, well disciplined, and well equipped, while the town dwellers were weak in all these respects and would usually try to flee once the siege went against them. Fallen towns were then mercilessly looted and the inhabitants killed or enslaved.

After the campaign and the distribution of booty by the leaders, the army disbanded. Leaders of various territorial ethnic groups swore allegiance to the king and arranged for the next campaign to be held so many days hence. At that time, criers were sent around to local markets stating the date and place of rendezvous for the army. Able bodied men were expected to go or send a representative bearing arms. A wife or female slave often accompanied each man to cook for him. But local townspeople were also expected to supply the army with food when it passed through their territory. However, it was preferred that the army be self-sufficient even to the point of digging their own wells. Discipline obviously posed some problems since the records indicate that at times army morale was low, especially during long, arduous campaigns. However, it picked up very quickly when the prospect of booty was in evidence.

The Nineteenth Century Kingdom

From the beginning of the nineteenth century our records and understanding of Bornu society increased enormously mostly because of the availability of excellent first-hand accounts such as those by Denham and Clapperton in the 1820s, Barth in the 1850s, and Nachtigal in the 1880s. When put together with the oral traditions these accounts fill out a fairly complete picture of Bornu society during the last century.

In the early part of the century Bornu political life was complicated by a fiction. The ancient Sefuwa rulers were still holding court while the Kanembu Shehus were in strict control of the state. This meant that many of the ancient titles lost their meaning because their functions were taken over by members of the Shehu's following. For example, the title of Kaigama, associated traditionally with leadership of the army while on a campaign, was dropped. Instead the Shehu used the title of Kachella, which had previously meant a slave follower who bears arms. Under the Shehus, Kachellas became powerful leaders of armed regiments of their own followers, the size of each Kachella's force being an indicator of his power and rank. At the same time the idea of raising military levies from fiefs was not dropped. Nevertheless the structure had changed, for now the Shehus used Kachellas and their permanent armed following as the military core of the state. Much later in the century, after the collapse of the Sefuwa dynasty, the title of Kaigama or war leader reappeared and was applied to the most powerful of these Kachella. In other words, a number of the old titles of Bornu could not be used in the nineteenth century, since at its beginning these titles were still associated with the old dynasty and its ancient court.

Although titles were varied to some extent, and new ones connected to the names of loyal followers of the Shehu appeared during the double regency, the Shehus organized their governmental administration in somewhat the same manner as that of the earlier Bornu state. The idea of the four quadrants atrophied while the old quadrant leaders remained under the ancient dynasty; and, as in the case of the war leader, these titles were not utilized until the old dynasty had been done away with. They were then absorbed into the general hierarchy of titles of those closely associated with the Shehu. However, the general idea of administering through quadrants was never used again. The Shehu's court met every day to discuss state matters and adjudicate cases when necessary. The Shehu sat on a raised dais and behind him in a semi-circle sat the male members of the royal family who were eligible for the throne. Sitting facing one another in two parallel lines in front of the group were nobles of the realm, slave and free, except for the Galidi-

THE NINETEENTH CENTURY KINGDOM · 25

ma, who when he was in court, sat in front of the throne facing the same way as the Shehu between the two lines. This symbolized his semi-independent status as a holder of a large section of the kingdom rather than a set of fragmented fiefs. Thus the idea of a consolidated set of fief-holdings on the western boundary was maintained. There was a constant threat from the Fulani which made such a move politically expedient.

How much actual power this nineteenth-century court actually had is debatable. Obviously a few favorite advisers who had the ear of the monarch could become very powerful men during the period of their favor. However, who these were seems to have varied throughout the century. Indeed even a place in court might be gained by a very ambitious rural chief, if he appeared often enough and was able to please the monarch by his service and tributes. In the realm of the judiciary some significant changes occurred as well. Before the nineteenth century, as we have already noted, there was a chief judge, the Talba, who was ranked as "the second man" in the state. During the double regency at the beginning of the century, the first Shehu, Laminu, acted as his own chief judge. He was steeped in Koranic learning and is supposed to have had magical powers that enabled him to adjudicate even the most difficult of cases, harshly but with justice. Parenthetically, this power—and not his military acumen and leadership—is considered by the traditions to have been the chief reason why Laminu saved Bornu from the Fulani wars. Later in his rule, sometime in the 1820s, Shehu Laminu appointed two leading religious personages who came from the families of the leading Bornu religious practitioners to the new offices of Liman and Imam. The former took over the major duties of chief legal adviser to the Shehu, while the Imam became the chief religious practitioner in the state. The old Talba stayed with the court of the former dynasty, and after its demise the title became a lesser one in the judicial hierarchy which is where it stands today.

Punishments for misdemeanors were relatively harsh by contempory standards. Adultery on a Muslim holy day could bring 400 lashes to a man or 200 to a woman. It was believed that judges in the capital of Kuka actually set spies upon the populace in search of law breakers. Intentional murder was punishable by death, and the relatives of the dead man carried out the execution by stoning the murderer. Thieves who were repeatedly caught finally had a hand cut off or were tortured by being buried up to the neck, then having their heads buttered or honeyed and exposed above the ground to attract insects. Unpaid debts proven in court resulted in the confiscation of all the debtor's movable property and a fine to the court. The debtor was pinned to the ground by court officials until he consented to confiscation. However, if he obviously had no means at all, the judge dismissed the case with the words, "God send you the means."

All titled officials and even untitled followers of the Shehu could be given or they could inherit, at the pleasure of the Shehu, rights of revenue collection and administration in one or more settlements spread throughout the entire state. These fiefs were granted by the Shehu, nominal owner of all the land in the state. Generally speaking such rights were hereditary in the male line, but the Shehu could diminish or expand the holding of one fief-holder at the expense of another, and a new monarch was expected to patronize his own favorites. Any person holding a fief directly from the monarch was called a chima kura or "the big lord." There were two types of differently named fiefs, the one where membership was territorially based, and the other where membership was ethnic or clan based, that is, based on birth into a particular group regardless of its territoriality. The big lord remained in the capital and administered his various fiefs, sometimes ranging up to twenty or more through his representative, the chima gana, or "the junior lords." Each junior lord lived in one of the fiefs of his superior, the fief-holder, or big lord. This junior lord was the highest authority living in the fief and from him one could appeal to the Shehu, being presented by representatives of the junior lord to the big lord living in the capital, and through this latter person to the court of the monarch.

This central administration was linked up to a local one. There was a village head, or bullama, who usually belonged to the male line of the founder of the settlement. However, he was only one among a group of eligibles. If the local junior lord did not like him or the tributes he delivered, then the junior lord could appoint another member of the same line. There are also some records of junior lords shifting the headship to other lineages as well as to persons within the same lineage. As settlements grew in size, sons, clients, and even slaves of the original village head would hive off and form small settlements or satellite communities nearby under the general jurisdiction of the original village head and the local leadership of the founder of the satellite community. These new heads were called mbarma (hamlet heads) as were heads of sub-sections of the original village that had some sort of unity based on occupation or kinship or a combination of both. Thus a big lord with the help of his junior lords could have his fief-holdings expand in size, and he tried to help this process along by not being too excessive in his demands on the peasants, and by protecting them from raiders and other forms of outside depredation. A big lord's wealth and ability to supply militia to the monarch depended upon his success as a fief-holder, so that it was in his best interests to see to it that each fief was well governed. People could complain to other nobles, or emigrate out of the fief, and such indications of mismanagement, if they continued, could lead to the granting of fief rights to someone else. This new big lord could then take over part of the original holding, or in extreme cases the entire fief was transferred to another big lord's administration.

A very successful village head—one with a large and flourishing settlement containing many satellite communities—could be rewarded for his increase in power and authority by being brought to the Shehu's court in the capital and given the title of lawan. The Shehu then performed a ceremony in which a turban was placed on the new lawan's head. This meant he was now a member, albeit a local one, of the titled nobility of the state. In this case, he not only paid accession-to-office-gifts to the junior and senior lord which all local headsmen did, but to the Shehu as well. Once having been advanced from bullama to lawan, it was now possible for some of the leading heads of satellite villages to be made into bullama (by the junior lord and the lawan) with their own mbarma or leaders of satellite communties under them in turn. If these inter-related communities developed even further, the lawan might be brought into the capital again and be made officially into an ajia by the Shehu, giving bullama and mbarma under him the opportunity of becoming lawan with bullama and mbarma in turn under them, all under final authority of the ajia and the most senior of the junior lords. By this time the big

lord living in the capital would have appointed several representatives to this particular fief because it had grown so big. Such fiefs were the ones most likely to fall
prey to sub-division at the death of a king and appointment of a new one. For at
this time the incoming monarch had to reward his chief supporters with grants of
new fiefs.

As in the pre-nineteenth century the political hierarchy served as an appeal
court system, and at the very top of the local fief hierarchy the junior lords shared
adjudication with the most senior local leader whatever his rank. Usually these very
senior political leaders of the fief had koranic scholars, or mallams, who gave legal
advice. Serious cases such as homicide were referred immediately to the capital.

The other variety of fief, that based on birth into a particular group, or *jili*
is less well understood. The word "jili" refers to variety or kind. The people speak
of this or that jili of soil, or tree, or person. In using it to refer to a person they
give his territorial or settlement background, or ethnic group, or his clan grouping
if this differs from his territorial classification. Thus a person can have several jili
—ethnic, territorial, or clan. Even patrilineal lineage affiliation can be described
under this term. Nomadic groups in Bornu were represented as jili in the Shehu's
court by a big lord of the jili (chima kura jilibe) ; this man was, in effect, the fief-
holder responsible for the nomad group. Sometimes he was a leader of the group
itself, and at other times he was a trusted Kanuri follower of the monarch. In both
cases the big lord of the jili administered the group through his own representative
in the group who was, unlike the territorial grouping, the local leader of a nomad
clan, or a sub-tribe. Sometimes entire tribal groupings came under one jurisdiction,
and at other times or in other sections of the state the tribe would be broken down
into subsections based on clan groupings with one or more clans under a single
fief-holder or big lord of the jili.

This double fief system allowed the nineteenth-century Bornu government
the organizational means of administering both the settled and nomadic populations of Bornu. It also did something else very important, for it allowed the government effective control over the population even when natural disasters such as
outbreaks of disease or sudden invasions sent the people into flight. If a large set
of settlements had grown up in one territory from an original one, and this area
was then beset by some disaster, which made the people flee in several directions,
they were still thought of as a jili or a single variety of persons. They were still organized under their old lords, and their old leaders still retained over them some
powers of taxation and demands of loyalty. If the entire kingdom was in an uproar
—as it was during the Fulani wars at the beginning of the century with people
fleeing in all directions—then old leaders, or former leaders, could muster their
scattered followers as jili, and the political integration of the kingdom remained
intact and viable until new settlements stabilized locally, and the territorial-based
fief system could re-assert itself.

Complicating the system was the settlement of groups with fiefs through
permission granted by the big lord in the capital. He could be approached by the leaders of a group of craftsmen, or kinsmen, or people of the same ethnic extraction,
who requested of him that they be allowed to settle in one of his fiefs. In this case,
the special group was directly under the jurisdiction of the lord through his local
administrator, the junior lord, who dealt with their headman. In later generations,

they often became a separate fief, or in some cases were absorbed into the territorial organization of the original fief. Again, the big lord might also settle some of his slaves in the fief, or he might ask to settle them in someone else's fief, or be asked by some other high ranking person if he would allow slaves to be settled in one of his own fiefs. Slaves delivered the results of their work on the land, and in craft-work directly to their own master whether this was the big lord of the fief or not. If they were in someone else's fief, presents were sent by their master to the senior fief-holder—the big lord—in the capital. It was also possible for the monarch or the big lord to settle holy men, men learned in the Koran, on a fief and such settlements were generally tax free.

There were two main taxes and innumerable smaller ones. Indeed, in the Kanuri language it is possible to denote the meaning of taxation, a tax on something, by simply adding the suffix "ram" to the activity or the object. Of the two main annual taxes, collected after the harvest, one went to the fief-holder and the other to the Shehu. The big lord collected tax on the basis of assessment of local produce by a special tax messenger who went out to the fief and after conferring with local leaders agreed on the tax. All who cooperated in tax collection kept some for themselves, passing surpluses on up the hierarchy to the big lord. In turn the fief-holder always gave gifts to the ruler upon receipt of their own fief-holder tax. Each year the Shehu appointed his own tax messengers from among the nobility and collected a royal tithe from the various fiefs. These men might and might not be fief-holders in their own right, but very often they were not collecting in their own fiefs. Other taxes were annual fees to local headmen, fees for clearing new land, for using new market space, for adjudication, for craftwork, for irrigation (where present), for extending any kind of privilege, etc. The system was essentially the same for the nomad groups, but one related complication should be noted. The people from dispersed localities owed some small taxation privileges to their previous headmen, even though they now lived in new settlements within new fiefs and were required to pay major taxes to their new settlement leaders.

One final point about the pre-colonial political system should be made. To understand such a kingdom it is necessary to keep distinct at all times the concept of a title from that of an office. The Kanuri kingdom had great rosters of noble titles that through time varied in number, numbers of holders per title, and the name of title. Some pre-nineteenth century titles such as the *Fufuma* or lord of the ancient capital city of Birni Ngazargamo dropped out of use. There were a number of men entitled Shettima while there was only one Digma or one Yerima. The titles are honorific, and even personal names which were attached to originally powerful households have become titles during Bornu's long history. Titles embellish a man' political duties, and even provide some opportunities for furthering his ambitions if their past history, or the activities of a title holder, enable him to manipulate the situation successfully for his own advancement. Offices on the other hand are positions in government giving the incumbent rights, duties, and obligations. An office may almost completely coincide with the title, as in the case of the ancient monarch whose title was Mai for probably a thousand years, and Shehu for the last century and a half. Or again offices can vary independently of titles. Thus the title of Digma which was held by a man with many official duties and much power in the mid-nineteenth century had changed by the end of the century, and the man holding this title had very few of these offices left—they were now the rights of persons holding quite different titles.

The economy of Bornu was a semi-specialized one. Almost everyone grew some crops, except a few cattle nomads, but at the same time during the long dry season people carried on craftwork, trade, and other specialized activities, such as providing medical or barbering services, or entertainment for those who were willing to pay. Everyone had access to new land, over which a person might establish ownership by his act of clearing it. If he used the land for only a few years, and stopped, then the land passed back into bush with no owner. Continued long-term use, especially that involving inheritance, meant that the owner could do with it what he pleased and transfer it to whomever he pleased. In other words the Kanuri had property concepts of usufruct or use-right, but they also had notions of freehold or private property in which land could be transferred by an individual after he had used it for a long time, or it had been passed on to his heirs.

The people raised specialized crops in the kingdom and practiced a myriad of different crafts. Each local craft was organized into a craft guild that helped set production and price standards under a local craft leader who benefited economically from his position and tried to pass it down through the male line. Markets, too, were under headmen and all goods to be traded went to weekly markets to which came thousands of people from the surrounding area.

Trade was accomplished by barter for the most part, although several forms of currency developed, which can be called special purpose or limited purpose money. For various kinds of trade, and within limits, certain objects—a man's robe, iron bars, slaves, horses, cotton rolls, Maria Theresa dollars, and other items—could be used. The trans-Saharan trader came to Bornu for slaves; he therefore demanded payment in slaves, and slaves became a kind of currency for this trade. People from Bornu traded south of Lake Chad for iron bars. These bars could be used to purchase anything in the markets southeast of Bornu where they were the chief export commodity. The same thing is true of cloth in the southern areas of Bornu where it was manufactured and where it was a major export item. Cloth rolls purchased any number of commodities from Bornu but only in that north-south trade. Cowrie shells came very late to Bornu (1820–1850) and never achieved the success as currency that they did elsewhere.

Another and important method of distribution of goods was carried out within the political system itself. Political superiors gave out enormous quantities of cloth, food, horses, and robes on particular holy days or special events such as rites of passage, or wrestling matches. On one occasion a witness in the early part of the century watched the Shehu give away more than a thousand men's robes and an equal number of bullocks and sheep. Although one would expect the leaders to give more than other men, they also served as a model for the population so that the amount of distribution actually carried on in this way must have been very great indeed.

Another important facet of the economy was foreign trade. Although the famous trans-Saharan caravans are supposed to have declined during the nineteenth century, by all accounts they were still of considerable importance for Bornu. Into Bornu came calico, cotton prints, fine silk, sword blades, writing paper, looking glasses, needles, razors, scissors, knives, cheap jewelry, and guns mostly from Europe. From North African manufacturers came cloaks, shawls, red felt and embroidered hats for men, sashes, trousers, carpets, religious books, spices, perfumes, and later, cowrie shells. From the desert came tobacco, barley, wild rice, dates, salt, natron, camels, and various assorted medicines, especially *drupa,* a herb believed to induce fertility in women. In return Bornu sent back sewn cloth, hides, leatherwork, sandals, feathers, ivory, gum arabic, Korans, kola nuts, and, above all, slaves. Caravans were large, and the trip was long, arduous, and dangerous because of the desert and its marauding inhabitants. However, just how important foreign trade was in the area is difficult to assess. The ordinary man probably used very little of outside manufacture, but at the capital such goods were considered necessities for people having any pretentions to higher status in the kingdom.

The Colonial Change

Using this description of pre-colonial Bornu it is now possible to discuss the kind of changes that were brought into the area by the inception of British rule at the beginning of the twentieth century. The British came to Bornu in 1901, after it had been occupied for seven years by Rabeh who had been intent on making himself the founder of its third dynasty. The British had not only to bring Bornu under the Northern Nigerian Government but to resuscitate its leaders who had not been in control of the area since 1893. At first they simply left the Shehu to do as he pleased, with the exception of waging war and carrying on the slave trade, which they vigorously put down. However, the idea of fiefs being ruled by lords at the capital seemed grossly inefficient, and they soon ordered that the Shehu choose his best fief-holders and that these be sent out to the locality of their fiefs to govern. Furthermore they decided to consolidate numbers of fiefs into larger units which they now called districts. There followed a tussle between the British and the Kanuri over how many village areas and how many districts there were going to be, the British generally trying to limit the number while the Shehu and his advisers generally tried to increase them. Finally a number around twenty was worked out for the districts and then village areas were incorporated into them. In general these village areas approximate the size and location of former fiefs. However the Kanuri felt that the head of a district was like a titled, local, territorial chief of the nineteenth century who has control over a large number of settlements, so he was called *ajia,* which translates today as a district head. Under him were heads of village areas that included a number of satellite settlements—and this village area head was—like the *ajia,* appointed and turbaned by the Shehu. He was therefore called a lawan (village area head) as was the titled head of a settlement with satellites during the nineteenth century. The difference, however, was that now there was no fief-holder or his representative to whom the local headmen were accountable. The district head held his office directly under the Shehu and the village area heads were directly under the district head. Small wards and hamlets were now headed up by bullama and the term for a bullama's subordinate, the mbarma, fell into disuse and has almost disappeared.

The mode of appointing and maintaining these jobs led to problems which were never really solved. The Shehu put up names for the district heads who be-

came a very powerful group of chiefs through whom the kingdom was administered. When these men went to their districts, sometimes they had precolonial ties
in these areas as big lords—some of the constituent towns in the district were their
former fiefs; sometimes however they were complete strangers to the area. Besides
this there was a constant shuffling of different district heads through transfers, dis-
missals, retirements, and deaths. The various village area heads under each district
head were chosen on the basis of investigations conducted by the British colonial
officials to find out who among the population had the hereditary right to leadership for a particular local settlement and its satellite communities. Very often there
was no tie of previous loyalty between the village area head and the new district
head. Previously the problem had been solved by sending out a chima gana or junior lord who represented the fief-holder. He had lived in the fief and created a set
of loyal local followers. At first district heads did the same things. They sent out
their own representatives—now called chima—to run the village areas in their district for them. This practice was soon discovered by the British and as early as 1910
was declared illegal, although it continued on until well into the 1930s, and there
are even some district heads today who admit they use chima to ensure control of
their district. In Chapter 6 we will take up this problem again and examine it in
more detail within the organization of the district.

The central government of the emirate has undergone a number of
significant changes under colonialism. At first the Shehu collected taxes on settled
peoples through the district heads and taxes on nomads through two trusted slave
nobles. This proved unsatisfactory to the British who very early in the century changed
the system so that each district head was responsible for tax collection on both settled
and on nomad populations in his district. This weakened the power of the Shehu,
but at the same time (ca. 1914) the British began enforcing among themselves the
idea that they must deal with the Bornu government through the Shehu and his
Council. Thus good or bad reports of the district heads or village area heads had to
be officially put through the Shehu giving him a great deal of either protective or
punitive power over his district and village chiefs.

After 1914 there was an increasing effort to create a working Council for
the Shehu with a modern treasury from which local planning could be financed.
Starting with only a few members it has grown slowly through the years to function as a cabinet with a Waziri or chief minister at its helm. Each councilor has a
portfolio or Native Authority department, such as Education, Works, Agriculture,
and so on, and these have central offices in the capital with representatives spread
out in district capitals throughout Bornu. The experience in this twentieth-century
emirate has produced Kanuri who now take part in regional and national politics
so that men from Bornu sit in Kaduna, Lagos, London, and even at the United
Nations in New York.

The movement of fief-holders out into the bush to administer districts produced a district capital where the ajia or district head resides. To this capital he
brought his urban followers; and to the village as well came the district judge and
his retinue. As the Native Authority departments developed, local representatives
of the various civil service departments of the emirate government came out to the
district capital as well. This makes the district capital a more complex and urban-
ized center and has forced the effects of such urbanization to spread widely

throughout the emirate. Roads were built connecting the district capitals to Maiduguri, the major city of Bornu and to one another, and district capital markets came to be among the most active because of the increased population in the district capitals not producing their own goods.

In the economic sphere the colonial era sounded a death knell for the Saharan trade. A dribble of caravan trade still exists, but it was the express policy of the British to face Bornu around and turn its trade toward Nigeria and the Nigerian ports. Caravans were heavily taxed, and European trading companies were encouraged to move into Bornu and start circulating cash and cheap import goods. These few large English and French trading companies encouraged the appearance of a corps of Levantine traders who are ubiquitous in West Africa. They take credit from the large companies, giving it out again to large numbers of Africans who buy and sell for them. By the second world war ground-nuts were a well established cash crop, marketed through these companies although controlled by the government. When inflationary boom prices for ground-nuts hit Bornu after the war, the people were ready to take full advantage of it and there was a surge upwards of consumer buying, so that radios, bicycles, and many other industrial commodities became part of local life. On the other hand, judging by the surprise registered in the annual reports of the colonical officials, the government was a little stunned at first to know what to do with its increased revenues. However a host of new improvements began to be an accepted part of life in the public sector, just as new import items became common to the private sector. The most recent of such changes has already been mentioned in Chapter 1. After independence, the digging of deep wells increased the cattle population enormously and has provided a basis for further development in the area. This, then, is the Bornu background. It is a long and eventful one—and the people are proud of it. For an anthropologist, one of the most intriguing questions to ask is "why"—why has Bornu lasted so long in this area? Why has it adapted so well to modern times? It has absorbed Shehu Laminu's destruction of the Sefuwa dynasty, Rabeh's conquest, the colonial overlordship, and national independence in its calm stride. Its leaders and its people are remarkably stable—yet not enslaved by tradition. Indeed they strive to change and develop Bornu and their future is a bright and hopeful one. In the chapters to follow I hope to provide answers to these questions in order that we may ask them again after considering in more detail the quality of life in Bornu.

3

The Family and Household
in Bornu

AFTER SUMMARIZING the historical background and the setting of Kanuri life, I can now proceed to analyze the society as a working, on-going whole, in other words as a process. Anthropologists generally do this by dividing the society up into what they consider to be its most significant parts. They then describe each part and try to show how these parts are related to one another, and to the functioning of a whole society. The manner in which such an analysis proceeds—what is left out, what is included, and what comes first or last—is the product of the author's "functional theory" of the society, his idea of how it works.

For Kanuri society I have chosen to start with kinship and the household as the first parts of the whole to be described and understood. First, the household is where the Kanuri themselves begin to learn of their own society and how they must act to become full-fledged participants. Secondly these parts, especially that of the household, form the basic units of Kanuri social structure such that almost all other social life in Bornu can be analyzed and understood once these particular parts are described. To start with a description of any other part of the society such as the economic or the political organization would require explanations and references to family and household life in order to make the material understandable to the reader. It is better to start the analysis at this point—that of kinship and household—then proceed to build up a picture of the society having first looked at what I consider to be its crucible, the kinship system, and its cornerstone, the household.

The Kinship System

The kinship system of any society involves three categories of behavior that may overlap one another but are always different from each other. They are as follows:

(a) Genealogical relations—the links between individuals which are based upon biological reproduction.

(b) Descent relations—the links between individuals which are based upon

33

the allocation of members in a genealogy to a socially and culturally recognized kin group. This may include the same persons as a genealogical group, or it may include only part of them.

(c) Affinal relations—the links between individuals which are based upon marriage through the socially recognized union of a husband and wife.

The Kanuri separate genealogical relations from those of descent just as we do by speaking of distant relations. They have a special word for such people, although many younger people today do not use it, and simply describe such people as "distant" or "far away" in the same way that Kano is far away from Maiduguri. The traditional word refers to a vine that grows around a household wall and then continues to reach out and grow on the walls of adjoining households. However the vines all stem from one root, just as an expanded genealogical tree can be viewed as coming from one man and his wife or wives. These distant kin do not attend one another's family ceremonies or send gifts on important occasions. Indeed their whereabouts are often not very well known to the person speaking of them. Many Kanuri can give quite a large number of such kin especially in their parents' generation, their own, and that of their children. On the other hand, like Americans, they find it difficult to remember relatives back beyond their grandparents even though there is a special kinship term for great-grandparents, and only a few people can name the brothers and sisters of their grandparents. Exceptions to this occur in increasing degree as families become more and more aristocratic. Such families retain the memory of important male ancestors in their genealogy much further back than do ordinary people; indeed they often maintain special persons to keep the memory alive.

Set into the genealogy of any Kanuri individual is his own descent group. In anthropological jargon—used because once understood, it is technically efficient—this group is reckoned cognatically with an agnatic emphasis. That is to say, Kanuri descent groups are based upon an individual's relation to persons through both his father and mother (cognatic relationships) ; and a person feels equally related to all of his four grandparents. However there is an emphasis placed upon those related to a person through males only (agnatic or patrilineal descent) for a number of important activities. The father's cognatic descent group is called the family of the blood, and the mother's cognatic group is the family of the milk, while the word "family" (dur) refers to both father's and mother's side of the family. Other evidence for the cognatic quality can be seen in the words used for various relatives in the descent group. There are no distinctions between mother's side and father's side in the terms for great-grandparent and grandparent, and although there are significant differences in the terms used to refer to relatives of the parent's generation level, cousins on both mother's and father's sides can be lumped under one term, which is the same as the one used to refer to a brother or a sister. On the other hand, there are differences between the mother's and the father's side which we refer to as an agnatic emphasis.

This emphasis can be easily seen in inheritance and when a man goes to court. The Kanuri follow Islamic inheritance law in which men receive two portions to every one given to a woman. Thus it is twice as important to be related to your father as your mother, if everything else is equal, such as the amount of wealth to be inherited and so on. These rules of inheritance are followed very closely in practice, because everyone knows that any dispute over inheritance that cannot be settled amicably between the surviving relatives goes to court—and the court normally takes ten percent of the estate for its adjudication services in an inheritance dispute. When a man is called into the courts, and most Kanuri have been to court at some time in their lives, he must go with his agnates—his father, paternal grandfather, father's brothers, sons, father's brother's sons, and any other male he can muster who is related to him in the male line. This agnatically related group is legally responsible as a whole for the acts of each of its members unless a crime against the state has been committed. A Kanuri who is threatened immediately thinks of this group as the one that he can turn to for help. As we shall see later the group often lives close together so that the agnates are neighbors as well as a corporate group in the eyes of the law. They help one another in many day-to-day activities, perform ceremonies together, and often practice the same or closely related occupations.

Although there is an emphasis on a person's agnates, his kin relations through his mother are also quite important. People who have no matrilateral kin (those related to a person through the mother), or very few of them, are considered to be unfortunate because they lack that much warmth and affection in their lives. These kin, say the Kanuri, love you like a mother loves her child. You can feel at home with them in a way that is less conflict-ridden than any other kinship relation. People often said that if they had to borrow money it was better to go to mother's kin first before asking anyone related to them agnatically. There is always some tension over property among an agnatic descent group because it is the major one for purposes of inheritance, family wealth, and privileges. People say that if a man borrows from his father or his father's brothers, or his brothers, or his patrilateral cousin, he is trying to get his inheritance or that of his brothers before the proper time. Furthermore, the responsibility in court, and in the eyes of public opinion, of one agnate for another also increases the tensions in this group as compared to the matrilateral one. By contrast, however, a man with no agnates is not just unfortunate—he is a social outcast. He has no group to stand up for him as a result of his birth into society; he has no legal right to a father's inheritance, he is thought of as an outcast, he must rely solely on his wits, and he cannot easily be trusted.

A village area chief and his advisers declared that I should not hire a certain man and claimed that they were going to see to it that I certainly did not take him into my household. They told me that no one in the vicinity knew his brothers or his father, or his father's brothers, or indeed if he had any, or where they might be, and he would not volunteer any information on the subject. In their eyes he was not a responsible person, and if he did anything wrong there was no group they could call into account for it. Unless he could attach himself to a household, he simply had no means of achieving an accepted position in the community, and the village leaders did not like the idea of making me, a European stranger, responsible for this unknown man.[1] Obviously under such circumstances illegitimate

---

[1] This would mean that as his household head I must appear in court if and when he did something wrong. The local leaders did not believe they could require this responsibility from me, and were thus faced with the problem of allowing into their community a man for whom no one could vouch, yet giving him a paid place in one of its wealthiest households.

children are abhorred and every effort is made to get the woman married should she be pregnant. Although her shame is great, it is nothing compared to the problems that the new individual will encounter unless people come to accept his mother's agnatic kin group as his—and whether that group will in fact accept him as a member. The pariah status of illegitimate children is easily seen in the widespread belief that they can only marry others like themselves or people of slave status.

So much then for the first two features of kinship, those of genealogy and descent. The third aspect, that of marriage relations, brings us much closer to what is commonly thought of as family life in western society. Using the anthropological jargon, we can sum up the kinds of relations invoked by a Kanuri marriage by saying that Kanuri marriage is polygynous with virilocal residence patterns which have a patrilocal emphasis and an exceptionally high divorce rate. In plain English this means that the men can marry more than one wife, up to four by Islamic law (they are polygynous); the wife invariably leaves her home to go and live with her husband in a place chosen by him (they are virilocal); and, this often but not always proves to be in the vicinity of, or even inside, the household of the husband's father (there is a tendency toward patrilocality). Finally, most Kanuri marriages, the vast majority of them certainly, end in divorce.

Because a marriage usually involves the creation of whole sets of kinship links where none existed before, the way in which such changes are brought about and made "official," or publically recognized, is an important aspect in the anthropological study of marriage. Furthermore, such activities are also very important moments in the lives of the individuals concerned, who must see to it that all that should be done is done correctly according to traditional custom. Thus we start looking at marriage by describing its inception.

In thinking about a marriage the first question that any Kanuri man asks himself is whether he can afford it or not. That is, can he and those people on whom he can count for financial aid take on the expense of a marriage ceremony and bridewealth payments; and, if he can, how high can he go?

A man who already has a wife or wives knows that he must give gifts, supposedly equal to those going to the bride, to wives already married to him. He knows that the pressures for expenditures for drummers, food, transportation of the bride to his dwelling, and many other aspects of the ceremony, will very likely involve more of an outlay than he can readily predict. Can the capital be raised for such an undertaking? Most men are helped by their friends, their kin, and their political and economic patrons if they have any. Kanuri recognize the outcome of marriage expenses in their oft-quoted saying, "A man who is not in debt over a wedding is a man who has no friends."

Bridewealth payments form the basic marriage expense, and they can vary in size and elaborateness depending upon the status of the two family groups who are joined through the marriage, the marital history of the girl, the previous relationship of the groom to the girl's family, the bargaining power of each party to the marriage arrangement, and the time of year during which the payments are to be made. Although other factors can enter in and pull the bridewealth up or down in individual cases, these are the most effective determinants of bridewealth.

The payments themselves can be divided into three general categories, plus a "rebate." First there are one or more small gifts given to the girl and her relatives, usually female relatives, in the name of the groom; these are called the *kwororam,* or the asking-a-question payments. Secondly, there are the formally recognized payments. The first of these is a large one called the *luwaliram,* given to the *luwali,* or the man who officially gives the bride to the groom and to whom she will return if she ever runs away or separates from her husband. This is followed several weeks later by a *sada'u,* a small fee given to the girl's family through her *luwali* on the morning of the wedding day. And thirdly there are a number of small payments paid out to the girl and her young friends, to the female relative(s) who accompany her to the groom's house, and to any unmarried sister she has left behind. The groom receives a few small gifts from the girl's family, and on the morning of the wedding day when the *sada'u* is paid, he receives gifts of money, clothes, and even on occasion a horse. He never knows beforehand, however, just how much or how little this "rebate" will come to in relation to his own outlay for the marriage.

When the status of the two families is similarly low, as it is in the vast majority of rural marriages, then there is very little worry over bridewealth. Generally it is not very high and almost standardized for the locality. An important man always pays more bridewealth because everyone believes he can afford it. Paying more for everything he does, including marriage, is one of the ways he validates or proves his higher social rank. An interesting insight is also gained when it is realized that not only is the status of the person getting married taken into account, but also the status of those whom he is associated with and whom he can count on for help. In our little town of Magumeri many people tried to have their daughters marry members of my household because, as they laughingly admitted, they knew I would help my household members with bridewealth, and my apparently wealthy status in Magumeri meant that payments could be set a good deal higher than usual for such a marriage.

No matter what the status of the two families may be, girls who have not been married before command a much higher set of bridewealth payments, and more of them. The magnitude is often three to five times as much and in extreme cases it goes even higher than that. Men tend to give more as they grow older and can afford it, while conversely women often receive less as they go from one marriage to the next. Kanuri say that a woman who has been married many times has been used a great deal and is therefore worth much less than others who have not had so many marriages and been used as much. On the other hand, if she remained with previous husband(s) for longer periods, has a reputation for quiet obedience, and staying inside the household, then the groom feels more confident about her and will pay more. Similarly if the women has borne children and has demonstrated her fertility, she is also worth more. Although some men know practically nothing about their wives to be, others investigate them and inquire into the reasons for previous marriage break-ups and so on. Was it because her previous husband beat her, or because she was an adulteress, or was excessively jealous of co-wives? Did she not perform her wifely duties properly, or show proper respect to her husband? Certainly some men like to know what kind of wife they are getting and this affects their willingness to pay bridewealth. However, it is not uncommon for a Kanuri man to say that he knew a particular wife for only a week, or perhaps just a day or two before they were married. In this case the woman's marital record is unimportant; instead the man considers other factors such as his need for a wife, the marriage expenses including the bridewealth, and the physical attractiveness of the woman.

The previous relationship of the groom to the girl and her family can vary the bridewealth enormously. Often the groom, and/or his family, are acquainted with the girl, and/or her family, as neighbors and friends. When this is the case, then other factors tend to enter in to determine the bridewealth. But in a number of special and not uncommon situations, the groom is released from the bulk of the bridewealth or it is substantially lowered. If the girl is his cousin (the Kanuri marry all cousins, although they claim it is not good to marry one's mother's sister's daughter) then he may find that only a small *sada'u* payment is necessary. About one-fifteenth of all Kanuri marriages are of this kind, and of these about one-fifth involve unions in which the little cousin was promised to the boy when she was an infant at the time that he was circumcised, roughly about puberty. At that time he becomes her *luwali* or the dispenser of her marriage rights and can arrange for her future husband or marry her himself when she reached puberty. In other cases the groom is a dependent or client of the girl's *luwali* (usually her father) and the marriage tends to cement the relationship between him and the father even further. Indeed many subordinates of "big men" in Bornu think of their superiors as being obliged to help them find a wife. In such a case the groom may assume only a small portion of the expenses, or the wife-to-be is a daughter or relative of the superior and the latter depresses the payments purposely, so his subordinate can marry. In a few cases girls are given to *mallams* (koranic teacher-priests) and no bridewealth is required. Such unions are called "marriages of charity" and the *luwali* who abrogates his rights to bridewealth in this fashion is considered to be a pious man. In actual practice it is not very common. This is seen in the marriage histories of the *mallams* themselves who may have married once in five or six times this way but rarely more than that. *Mallams* claim that they do not like it because it makes them obligated to the wife-giver for free prayers, constant officiating as a religious leader in the household of the *luwali,* and so on, so that they avoid such charity in order to maintain their independence. This avoidance is mitigated if they are already members of the *luwali's* household and the marriage is simply cementing the relationship.

The bargaining abilities on both sides of the marriage can also determine the bridewealth. The groom's representatives are told by the girl's family, through her *luwali,* that the groom can expect many gifts which will compensate for an elaborate and expensive wedding. The groom's representatives tell the woman and her relatives, especially her *luwali,* of the groom's qualities, especially his kindness and generosity, his wealth and expectations of more, his potentialities as a successful man, and his connection through friends, through his own services, and relatives to very important people. On his side, the *luwali* speaks of the benefits to be gained by marriage to this particular girl and slowly the bridewealth payment, especially the *luwaliram,* emerges at a set price. On her first wedding night, a previously unmarried girl also bargains at great length in order to bid up a special consummation fee that is her right.

If the marriage arrangements take place in the autumn, or around harvest time, it is assumed that the man will have more cash than at other times. Thus the price at this time of year for nearly everything, including weddings and bride-wealth, goes up.

When all the exchanges are completed everyone participating in a wedding gets some present of money, food, and clothing. The *luwali,* especially at first marriages, gets the bulk of the bridewealth and distributes the rest to the girl's family both on her mother's and on her father's side. After the first marriage the girl tends to keep more and more of the bridewealth for herself, giving the *luwali* what amounts to a fee for serving as the official bride-giver. It is also important to note that when there are disputes between a husband and wife, the first person to whom both turn for arbitration is the *luwali.*

The Kanuri think of getting married in several ways. First of all they divide all marriages into first marriages (to take a girl or a small girl), and secondary marriages with a divorced woman (to take a woman or to take a divorced woman). First marriages take place for a girl around the time of puberty, while boys do not marry until they are in their late teens or early twenties, and young men of twenty-eight and twenty-nine who have not yet been married are not hard to find.

An interesting sidelight on marriage with previously unmarried young girls is the ambivalence men feel about it. Men obtain much prestige from such a marriage. But its cost invariably puts a man into great debt, and consummation of the marriage itself, traditionally, is a semi-public affair in which old women related to the girl sit outside the marriage hut and whisper to their newly-wed relative that she must resist the advances of her husband. They do this until very late at night or until they are given some proof of the girl's virginity by the husband. They then make a fearful clatter in the town or village to announce the premarital chastity of their young relative. Standards of personal appearance and sexual attraction are important to Kanuri men and center on more sexually mature women. Such standards deal with hair style, facial symmetry, type of walk, and other physical attributes and skills, as well as ability at wifely chores. None of these attributes are in any degree well-developed among young girls, so that the man must control himself and almost publicly proclaim his manhood and sexual prowess with a young girl who is not defined as sexually exciting by the culture. This causes much anxiety and I have seen men praying almost continually for several weeks in order to gain the strength to carry out a virgin's consummation. It is important to note that when some western educated Kanuri talk about marriage they immediately fasten on this semi-public consummation of the girl's first marriage as a custom that will be dropped in the future, and certainly one they do not intend to carry out or even allow in their lives. From the girl's point of view, as education in western-style schools becomes more common and the length of time in school increases, then the time of first marriage for the girls will move ahead. At present however there are only a handful of Kanuri girls who attend schools beyond the age of traditional marriage.

But what is the basis for the conflict? Why are men willing to suffer to gain such an unattractive wife? Men always explain it in the same way. A young girl has never been touched sexually by other men; he is the first; he can train her as he likes, and teach her to be a proper wife to suit his own personal wishes. Besides, it is a good Muslim custom, they always add, as they do about almost every custom when they are asked. In this case they are correct, for such young marriages are very widespread throughout the Islamic world. However there is more to it than that—indeed it comes close to the heart of the Kanuri way of looking at things. Kanuri social life is a constant search for fruitful social contacts in which one man is the superior and the other a subordinate to him. Between the sexes, the culture defines women as inferior in rank to men. Thus the place universally available to all men for the achievement of subordinates is the family and the household, and the ideal female subordinate is a young girl, one who has not yet been divorced, that is rejected her subordination to her husband, and one whom the husband can train to become properly obedient to his own personal wishes. Thus marriage to a previously unmarried girl symbolizes what every man wants, not sexually, but socially; unblemished and complete obedience from docile subordinates who receive material benefits in return for subordination. Seen in this light the marriage with young girls then becomes more understandable for it represents some of the most profoundly important values in the society.

Most Kanuri do not, however, marry girls who have never been married before. Generally they marry a *zower*—or divorced woman. This is carried out with much less ceremony than the virgin marriage. Men may see a divorced woman they like and simply send a friend who asks if she would like to marry. Or the men may begin an affair with her, give her market money once a week just as he would a wife, and then during this time decide whether or not he and this woman should proceed towards a marriage. Such liaisons are considered formally to be illegal extramarital relations, but in everyday life they are tolerated as a form of courtship. Harsh approbation is directed toward sexual relations by a man with another man's wife. Thus although a very few men claim to remain chaste in their relations with a divorced woman, most men agree that there is nothing seriously the matter with a discreet affair with such a person.

As Muslims the Kanuri also think of marriage as a relationship involving more or less *purdah,* or wifely confinement within the household. Generally, it is made quite clear before the marriage begins just how much constraint the husband expects. And for the most part such restrictions are positively related to the class and status of the husband. Thus the higher the status of the husband, the greater the probability of almost total confinement on the part of the wife. Certainly all Kanuri men would like their wives to remain inside the compound, however very few can afford to insist. To do so necessitates that there must be a well inside the compound, enough wealth so that the husband does not require the wife's work in the fields, and enough help so that he can send a male servant or client along with her on the few occasions when it becomes absolutely necessary for her to go out.

The Kanuri themselves categorize a few other forms of marriage on the basis of the relations already existing between the partners, or being set up by the marriage. They speak of cousin marriage, marriage with a religious practitioner, marriage with a wealthy or powerful person (a marriage of pleasure) as varieties of unions. They also mention the possibility of the sororate (marriage with a person called sister by one's dead wife) and the levirate (marriage by the younger brother of his dead brother's wife or wives). These latter are quite rare, and I have only recorded one case of the levirate in the last ten years, and none of the sororate. Kanuri think marriage with wife's sister, or person she calls sister while she is still alive (sororal polygyny) is an awesome idea, for it implies the sororate to them or wish for the death of a present wife.

In a few upper class households there are concubines who have the status of female slaves. These act as servants to the wives of the household and are used by the household head as sexual partners "any time you ask," as one informant put it. They are spoken of as being "half a wife." This refers to the fact that the husband gives them one half the amount of everything given to a wife. Generally they are too low in status to compete with the wives of the household unless they are considered exceptionally beautiful, or if they have given birth while the wife has not, and the child is recognized as that of the concubine. One informant very clearly explained his possession of concubines in economic terms. His household, he said, was very large, and he regularly fed twenty to forty people per day. This figure often increased to fifty or sixty on special occasions. The work of preparing so much food on time and regularly was simply too much for his wives, so he always has a number of concubines to help with the catering problems associated with his high status in the community.

Why do men want to get married? In answering this question men constantly reiterate cooking, food producing, and child-bearing. Cooking—to the unmarried man—is a most important point. Men never cook and if a man has no wife he must eat his food in the household of a relative or neighbor who is already married. This produces obligations by the unmarried man towards the married men which must be repaid with some service such as farm labor or running messages which signifies subordination. Thus a man with a wife can create obligation among unmarried men or at least avoid becoming obliged in this way to others. This is not, of course, the whole story. Women are also prized for their work in the fields. Indeed men estimate an annual increase or decrease in crop yield by referring, among other things, to the loss or gain of a wife.

Women on the other hand want wealth, although they often want freedom as well and more power in marriage than the culture allows for. This leads to trouble. But before we go into marriage itself, let us look at an actual case in which a man decides to marry.

Modu was twenty-six years old. He had been married twice; once for a period of nine months, then divorced and single again, then married a second time for a year and a half. In this he is no different from the vast majority (as high as eighty to ninety percent) of young Kanuri men his age. Now he was single again and living next door to his older-half-brother at whose house he was eating his meals. He wanted to take a wife and become independent of his older brother. He chose a new woman in the village about the same age as himself. She was visiting her elder brother who was a minor official in the district court. Minor though he was, his family was well-to-do and Modu was but a country peasant. The woman was beautiful and rather more sophisticated than local country girls, coming as she did from the city. Modu thought her most attractive in every way, even though gossip had it she had been married six or seven times.

Despite the gossip he decided to try and marry her, feeling that her past reputation made her available to the likes of him and not too costly in terms of bridewealth. Late one afternoon he sent over some kola nuts using an intermediary;

often people use old women for such purposes. He was anxious about the gift and so went to an expert on medicines who gave him a couple of special kola nuts whose magical love potion power would direct the woman to find him irresistible. His confidence thus buoyed up, he visited her himself and they had a short affair. He tasted her cooking, observed her behavior, and after two weeks sent a friend to the older brother to arrange for the marriage payments. Three weeks later, after the marriage was proposed to the *luwali,* (in this case her older brother), the couple were married. Modu was delighted and later assured me that for most of the entire six months they remained married he was quite happy. In the end they quarreled bitterly because his wife was out of the house visiting much too often for him not to be suspicious of her fidelity. Finally he simply told her to pack her things and leave his house.

The case illustrates the ease with which Kanuri men and women moved in and out of marriage—a perfectly normal pattern in Bornu. Bornu is a land where divorces are very common, and a marriage break-up is never the social and psychological catastrophy it can easily be in the west. To understand why we must look more closely at Kanuri married life.

Married Life

By comparison with western society, Kanuri husbands are at home a great deal. The home is the center of activities where men take their leisure, visit their friends, and receive visitors all day long. If at all possible they carry out their occupational activities in the household making it the central location for their daily work. Such constant contact of husband and wife in the household is rather rare in western society. Paradoxically however, husbands and wives are far less intimate and friendly than they are in the west. In their daily lives, women cook, nurse young children, bring water for the household if there is no well, help in the fields, grow garden crops and maize in the back of the compound, prepare cooked and uncooked foods, make pots, trade, and visit one another to help with the preparation of ceremonies as well as for companionship and hairdressing. Men clear the fields and plant crops, work at a large number of crafts including modern ones such as truck driving or using Singer sewing machines; they also engage in religious activities as specialists, and carry out specialized political, judicial and medical roles.

In upper class families, women are in *purdah* (restricted to the household) and live at the back of the compound furthest away from its entrance. They leave the compound only on rare occasions and even then they must seek the permission of their husbands well in advance. They are usually accompanied on such excursions by servants who may escort the upper class lady half way across the emirate to visit her own family for a ceremony at which her presence is required. On the other hand, peasant women must go to the well at least twice a day for water, and in some villages this means a walk of several miles. These women work on the farm plots of the various members of the household during the short growing season and sell cooked foods. Ordinary women use the occasions away from their husband's households to meet and talk freely with other women, and sometimes, of course, with other men.

For the most part relations between husbands and wives are highly formalized. They avoid using one another's names in conversation. In public only the most necessary interaction takes place between them when other people are around. Women walk generally behind their husbands when the two are going somewhere together, and even in the household the woman remains or should remain inside the compound. When he is not working, the husband sits most often in the entrance hut or in front of his household. A visit to a Kanuri household brings the husband to the entrance hut if he is inside, and at the same time the wife retreats out of sight. For the most part women remain in the company of women, and men with men. Only in a few rare cases have I ever observed public expressions of friendliness between a husband and a wife.

Cultural tradition has ordained that men are the dominant members of society, and women, more specifically wives, are to be submissive. This is both Islamic and Kanuri. It is good and seemly for a woman to obey her husband and to appear humble in his presence. Men decide where the family is to live, who a daughter is to marry, and a multitude of day-to-day questions on every aspect of family life. For a wife or indeed any family member to make a decision without consulting the husband-father is asking for trouble. Disputes between a husband and a wife, in which a man can refer to a breech of his authority as the cause of the disagreement, are invariably settled in his favor and might include physical punishment by the husband if the wife is very young. Thus a district head ruled against the plaintiffs in a case in which the husband had been accused by the wife's relatives of a beating which he had administered to her. The district head stated that the girl had been grossly disobedient and that it was the husband's right to punish such acts, especially in one so very young who was still learning how to be a proper wife.

One out of every two Kanuri marriages is a polygynous one. Thus a woman is very likely sometime during her life to be in a situation in which she is one of two or more co-wives. Relations between co-wives is governed by strict codes of procedure. Each wife has her own hut in the back area of the compound farthest from the entrance hut or gate. Each wife cooks her own food and raises her own children who sleep in her hut while they are small. When co-wives go abroad as a group to the wells or to a ceremony, the senior wife—the one married to the husband-in-common for the longest time—takes the lead with the other wives behind in a single file. Then come the female children in terms of their own relative ages. During a family ceremony the senior wife is the authoritative head of the women's section and directs the work of the others. Relations with the husband are strictly regulated. The general rule is that each wife performs her duties from sunset to sunset and the evening meal is taken after sunset. Every wife takes her own turn cooking the husband's food and that night she visits him in his hut. He may or may not have intercourse with her, but he must try to share sexual favors as equally as possible or else word about it will spread around in the family and cause tension between wives.

Although it is very rare to observe cases of long-standing co-wife relations because of the high amount of divorce in Bornu, the Kanuri always say that co-wives can become very good friends if they remain married to the same man for a long period of time. On the other hand it is fairly easy to observe co-wife relations that are stiff, formal, and even tense and hostile. One woman whom I know actually badgered her husband into marrying a young girl. He finally acceded to her wishes and chose a previously unmarried girl from a nearby village. The bride-wealth and marriage expenses sent the man into great debt, but he decided that it was worth it because of the increased prestige and because he believed his wife would now stop agitating him about it and have a young friend in the house that she said she had wanted for a long time. Only three weeks afterwards the senior wife began to to demand that the husband get rid of the new wife. "The young one was not helpful," she said, and she also accused the husband of favoring his new wife over her. Finally she threatened to leave if the new wife was not dis-posed of and the confused husband, worried over his debts, and angered because of her change in attitude let her go and divorced her rather than accede to her new demands. In another case a man announced to his wife that he was going to marry a new wife, and she flew into a towering rage which lasted for several days. She was only mildly contained by the many gifts and had several outbursts of temper during the wedding ceremony.

Although men are dominant by force of tradition, discrepancies are very common in everyday life. I have observed women leaving their husbands' com-pound against their wishes, and many are said to be unfaithful sexually. Indeed this is a favorite topic of conversation and men who are intimate friends tell jokes about who is having an affair with whose wife. Some women openly flaunt their husband's authority by threatening to leave him if he refuses to allow them their own way. In many cases such inconsistency between the expectations of husband and wife relations and the realities of everyday married life lead to divorce.

Only rare Kanuri have not been divorced once or twice during their life-time, and many have divorced three and often four times; eight or nine divorces is not uncommon. When explaining divorces, husbands complain of their wives cook-ing badly, or not on time, or not enough; they also complain of visits to relatives and friends that they felt were unnecessary, of attendance at public dances or cere-monies, of their wives being dirty, or of adultery; but always they mention and stress some activity that involves the wife's disobedience. Wives when speaking of di-vorces complain of their husband's intolerance, of their activities outside the house-hold, of their stinginess, or their lack of sexual attention or skill, or of their extra-marital affairs; sometimes they complain of co-wives, or the husband's lack of appreciation of their services, especially their cooking.

Most divorces occur in the first five years of marriage, and the husband al-most always formally initiates divorce proceedings. This results from the fact that the bridewealth must be returned if the wife officially initiates the divorce. Gener-ally speaking, women can informally initiate a divorce by behaving so badly that the husband has no recourse but to send her packing, thus forfeiting his bride-wealth and submitting to her wish. In one case I knew, the mother and older brother of the young girl instructed her to behave badly because they disapproved of her husband's wish to take her to the city. He took her anyway but by the end of a month found it impossible to live with her and had to send her back to her rela-tives in the rural area. In a few cases women initiate divorces rather more forceful-ly. A favorite technique in this regard is to grab the husband by the collar of his robe and scream at him, "I won't let go until you say, 'I divorce you.'" A crowd gathers and the man invariably then capitulates by saying, "I divorce you." In very rare circumstances women themselves initiate the proceedings by announcing the divorce, although this is usually done with a circumlocution such as when she says, as one woman did, "There is nothing holding us together but these gifts that you have given me. Take them. I wish to go."

About eighty to ninety percent of all marriages end in divorce, probably because it is such a simple affair. The husband in most cases simply tells the wife to go, saying "I divorce you." He does not say it three times, as is usual in Islamic countries, because the wife may return, for the Kanuri practice of Muslim marriage is such that, after saying "I divorce you," three times there should be no reconciliation or remarriage. Once a pronouncement of divorce has been made the woman leaves her husband's household and the marriage enters a special hundred-day period in which the woman cannot remarry although the man may do so. This is defined as a waiting period to see whether or not the woman is pregnant so that the man can claim the child. The woman generally returns to her *luwali* at this time and there is always some negotiation between the man and the *luwali* to see whether or not the marriage can be patched up. About one-third of all divorce pronouncements do end in reconciliation even though the husband most often divorces her again later on. It is interesting to note that unlike western society, practically no Kanuri divorce cases (perhaps one percent) go to the courts; thus it is impossible to get the records of divorce except through field study of actual cases.

When a divorce occurs children remain with their father unless they are still nursing. After nursing they are generally sent back to the father's household, although the period is sometimes stretched out for young girls who are trained by their mothers. Children of broken unions are cared for by a father's co-wife or by some other close relative of the father. Contacts with a divorced parent are always maintained and the child visits his or her mother regularly. This is especially true for boys who expect to take care of their mother when she is an elderly unmarried woman. Conflicts sometimes arise because a man's daughter does not return and the mother's relatives or one of her subsequent husbands might try to arrange a marriage without consulting her own father. If such consultations take place, however, no one feels put out and the man who arranged the marriage takes a portion of the bridewealth in payment.

Each spouse in a marriage maintains very close contacts with his or her own relatives. Presents are exchanged and visits back and forth between members of kin groups are very common. Children are named after relatives, especially grandparents, and in many cases go to live with them after weaning, or before the birth of a new baby in the family. Only in cases of long term marriage does a wife finally come to feel a part of and fully accepted by her husband's family. However when this does happen the wife can become a very powerful voice in the family, and her long and intimate association with her husband often means that she has become a permanent authority in the household. In one such case a senior wife had never been married to anyone else and had been married to her husband, a powerful man in the village, for thirty years. The man remarked that he made very few decisions without consulting this woman, and people recognized that she had a powerful position in village affairs. Such cases, however, are not common. Kanuri marriage involves a separation of the sexes not only by custom and tradition but as a result of the conflicts in marriage relations which produce tensions between husbands and wives and thus lead to frequent divorce. In such circumstances a close intimate relationship between husband and wife is a victory of personality over social and cultural conditions in the society.

Other Family Relations and the Behavior Norms

To the Kanuri themselves, family relations—those between parents and children, between siblings, uncles and nephews, grandparents and grandchild, between one in-law and another and so on—are part of a larger framework of behavior governing almost all the important relations between persons and groups in the society. The Kanuri believe that these relations originate in the family where the person first learns them and are then extended outwards to include all of the important social relations of adult life. From the anthropologist's point of view it is impossible to say which comes first. Do the family relations create or cause those social relations which best suit them, or does the society outside the family create the kind of family relations required by the society at large? Whatever the answer, the Kanuri are quite clear on this point. They believe that the rules governing social relations in the family and household are the essential guides to the successful operation of the larger scaled organizations in the economic and political life of their society. Thus many social relations in Bornu have a kin-like quality or are spoken of using the idiom of kinship, even though the persons involved clearly recognize that they have no kinship with one another through genealogical, descent group, or affinal relations.

The most important of these relations is the *barzum* or discipline-respect relationship closely modelled on, and usually spoken of in terms of, the father-son relationship. In this relationship a father gives his son protection, security, food and shelter, a place or status in the community, an occupation, helps him to arrange a marriage, and represents him in the adjudication of disputes. In his turn the son must be completely loyal, obedient and subserviant to his father, and work for him in whatever way the father feels is necessary. This respect is so demanding a mode of behavior in families that young children are sometimes sent away to a relative's household, usually to a grandparent, and return as one infomant put it, "when they understand respect." When the father dies, an older brother or a paternal uncle may take the place of the father as head of the household. He then receives the same respect from the dead man's children. This is so because they are older men with authority in the household. Thus all senior relatives, older siblings, and paternal uncles receive respect, and although it may not have the intense quality of the father-son relationship to begin with, everybody knows they may have to treat such a person as if he were a father under certain circumstances. Besides this, a young child is taught that in general older people are to be respected, no matter what their sex or degree of relationship to oneself. Other persons in society are indicated as being "like your father" or "greater than your father" in the amount of discipline and respect that they require. Religious specialists, political leaders, and any compound head with whom a person is staying are all in this category. In other words, the father-son behavior norm is the model used by the people themselves to describe the nature of all authority relations in the society.

Daughters are taught in the same way, but they must give great heed to their mothers who are, in a day-to-day sense, the authority figures in their lives. Although men will respond to questions by saying they have similar discipline and respect for both their father and mother, there is in addition an emotional quality to the mother-son relationship almost wholly lacking in that between the father and his children. For many Kanuri men this is leavened by the high divorce rate that separates them from a continual long-term association with their mothers. But for those who have had consistent long-term associations with their mothers this can be the strongest emotional relationship of an entire lifetime. Thus one young man resigned from a salaried job suddenly one day because, as he said, "I wanted to see my mother and felt she was too far away."

Discipline-respect relationships are qualified by another mode of behavior called *nungu,* or shame-avoidance. This means that the persons in the relationship, especially the junior, must be subdued, self-controlled and constantly be restricted in his behavior to very limited traditional patterns. In the extreme, people who have *nungu* relationships would not eat together from the same bowl, as friends do, and only the most necessary conversation passes between them, while the junior keeps his eyes lowered and is in no way informal. This is best seen when a very friendly person is suddenly confronted with, or is observed with, his own father. His jocularity suddenly disappears; he becomes extremely serious and humble, and never speaks until spoken to unless he has a particular message he has been commissioned to bring. Even then he will wait until asked to state the meassage.

Within the kinship system the epitomy of the *nungu* relationship is that of father and son, but other senior men like father's and mother's brothers as well as older brothers may all have some shame-avoidance in their relationship to a young nephew or brother. Such shame-avoidance increases when the age differences are greater, when the wealth and power of the senior is great, and most particularly if the senior has either taken the place of a dead father, or a young man has been sent to live with his senior male relative so that the older brother or uncle is now his compound head. When there are sex differences as well, then *nungu* is less intense within the descent group but more intense with affines to whom it applies. Thus a Kanuri man will tell his mother things he cannot speak of to his father, and generally he can speak more easily to his mother's and his father's sisters than he can to his uncles. However the most abject avoidance is maintained between in-laws of the opposite sex. Such persons would never allow themselves to be alone together; they avoid each other on a path (the woman steps out of the way with eyes downcast), and they would never speak to one another directly. Because Kanuri girls go to live with their husbands, often close to or in the households of their husband's family, then the burden of such avoidances falls on the bride. Only when the wife and husband move to a household of their own at some remove from that of his parents can the intense avoidance and tension generated by strict *nungu* rules between the young girl and her father-in-law be alleviated.

In the wider society there are *nungu* relations as well. Generally speaking, the greater the discipline-respect, the more likely it is to be associated with *nungu* or shame-avoidance. Thus the relationship between a man and his direct superior in a political or economic organization has many elements of *nungu* connected with it. He rarely speaks directly to his superior, they do not have long conversations, he mutters "yes, yes, yes" while his superior is talking but keeps his eyes cast downwards; to very powerful superiors like the Shehu he must not talk directly at all, but to an intermediary. Wives of such persons are treated like senior in-laws. Indeed, given the traditional practice of giving wives to clients, often from among one's own daughters, it is quite possible that the wife of a superior will one day become the mother-in-law of a client subordinate.

As a person grows up in his family, he also learns that there are some people with whom he can have very permissive relations. The ideal person is a grandparent, although a similar relationship exists between a spouse and all of his younger in-laws. A young boy can go to his grandfather's house and take things, pull his grandfather's beard, and generally misbehave, all the while receiving only a pat on the head for such licentiousness. Sex differences do not count here although there is sexual joking especially in the relations between a person and a junior in-law of the opposite sex. Later in life young boys and girls learn that such joking (*suli*) is a special form of interaction that can also be carried out between traditionally competitive occupational groups and traditionally hostile ethnic groups. On an individual basis one person in such a relationship calls the other "grandson" and the "grandson," being the younger, calls the older man "grandfather." The Kanuri explain that this helps to alleviate any tensions which may develop between the persons in such groups who are natural competitors or by tradition hostile to one another.

Finally, in the extended family and the household a young person grows up with brothers, sisters, and cousins who are also called siblings. The closer the age and interests of "siblings" of the same sex, the greater the solidarity and friendship. During childhood the young person usually chooses a young age-mate from amongst his siblings or cousins as his *ashirmanzə* or "secrets man," the person who knows his most intimate thoughts, hopes, and fears. Later in life, he chooses other *ashirmanzə* from inside his kinship network and outside it. He learns the faculty of intimacy, however, in his youthful friendships in the family and the household.

The family and the household then are orbits in which ways of behaving are learned and these characteristic norms of behavior are used for wider-scale social relations throughout the individual's life. At the core of these relations is *bərzum* discipline-respect. As well shall see, Bornu is an interwoven set of economic and political hierarchies, and this relationship of *bərzum* serves as the chief mechanism for the proper functioning of these complex relations between superiors and their subordinates.

The Household

Kinship may form the biological and the behavioral basis for Kanuri society, but it does not provide a place for such relations to operate. The Kanuri live in cities, villages, and hamlets and the basic unit of organization in these settlements is the household, rather than the family or any set of kinship groups. Even though these may be synonymous in some cases, in many compounds family and household are certainly not the same, and the distinction is fundamental to an understanding of the society. Furthermore the household, or compound as it is sometimes called, is stable in comparison to the family. The family can be split, and very often is, by divorce or death, or the movement of its members to a new place. While such changes occur, the household remains; its personnel may change, its landholdings may expand or contract, and its relations with other households through its household head may shift—but people see it as an organization in terms of which settlements are built into larger units; into wards, hamlets, villages, cities, and finally, the state itself.

The personnel of a household is based on that of the family, and generally moves through a cycle that may involve several alternatives to the usual pattern. Let us start with a couple. A young man marries for the first time, and in about sixty percent of the peasant cases recorded for three rural villages in Bornu, he brings his wife to the vicinity of his father's compound or moves into a section of his father's compound. If the latter is the case, he will move to his own compound close by after his own conjugal family (his wife or wives and children) increases in size either through the birth of children or the acquisition of more wives. When his own children grow up, his daughters leave to marry and return from time to time because of divorces or separation from their current spouses. Because many sons bring their wives to their father's household or close by, the original father finds himself the nominal head of a growing patrilocal extended family which, as we shall see in Chapter 6, can in time become a separate ward or sub-ward of the town. When the father dies, the oldest son or the most capable or successful of all sons takes over the compound of the dead father. Lands and goods are apportioned among the male heirs, although the person taking the father's role sometimes takes half the land and divides the rest equally among the living heirs. Thus in one case a man with three brothers took his father's fields and divided them in half. One-half he kept for himself, and the other half he split among the three brothers.

A problem that frequently emerges at this time is that of the mothers of half siblings—the wives of the dead man. The man who takes over his father's compound or household tends to install his own mother there as a dependent, since most old women are without husbands.[2] If she is a vigorous woman, she can become a powerful person in the household. Indeed in the royal household she has a special title, as we have seen, and was traditionally a noble-woman of great power. The other wives of the dead man must go and live with their own kinsmen, usually one of their sons. In one case this problem was intensified by the fact that the household head, a powerful political leader, had only one son and that by a concubine. When the present head dies, his senior wife, a woman of very powerful upper class affiliations will have to leave and her own slave—a woman very much junior to her—will be installed as the senior woman of the household. Such eventualities can cause tension between the members of any household who know that some day the power and authority relationships within the household will change hands.

In the same vein, siblings tend to drift apart after the death of their father. Even though they live close by one another, their unity and cooperation is not as great after the father's death as before. On the other hand, this can be ameliorated by social and economic factors which are important to keep in mind. Thus if a senior brother takes over a powerful political role, or a lucrative economic one, and

[2] As a woman approaches old age she finds it extremely difficult to remarry and thus most old women are resigned to being beyond the marriageable period of their lives.

uses it to benefit himself and his brother, the group tends to remain intact rather than break up. The following statement by an informant illustrates some of the forces at work in the continuity of a household organization that has gone on for more than one generation.

I did not have a father and was now living in the house of my elder brother who was head of the house. I therefore had to give my brother the same discipline-respect as a father and keep myself continually under his command. I wanted a wife. (All my other brothers had married and moved out to form their own households by now), but my brother ordered me to wait patiently until I learned the occupation (butchering) properly. He said, ". . . continue to stay in my house and carry grass for my horse and learn the butcher's trade, and I will feed you and give you money for spending and I will buy your clothes." But I was not happy and saved my money in secret, saved enough to take a wife of my own. They were cheap in those days. My older brother was angry and did not agree to the marriage for he still wanted me to stay in his compound. But I did not wish to do that, and so I moved away to a house that X, the husband of my mother's sister in Maiduguri owned here in the butcher's quarters.

The informant felt that his older brother was taking advantage of him and so he planned secretly to start up a household on his own. The brother might have kept him, had he been more generous and supplied a wife to his younger brother, as a really successful compound head would have under similar circumstances. Another informant, a money lender, had very little status because of his money-lending activities, but was the possessor of great wealth. He managed to keep his brothers near him and their sons and the wives of all of these plus a number of other people who he supported with loans, defended in the courts, and loaned money to for wives and for trading purposes. He arranged for their marriages and sometimes even obtained girls for them. On the other hand, they served him loyally as messengers, laborers, and loyal supporters in the community at large. A number of people, men and women, move completely away from former households when they get married and move out on their own. This depends basically on what advantage they see in it for themselves, and, in the city, on the availability of land and rent.

About forty percent of the ordinary peasant households have one or two unmarried adult men living in the compound who are not members of the family at all. They help the household head on his farm plots, carry grass for his horse, take messages for him to friends and relatives, carry his goods to market, learn his dry season non-farming occupation, and give him the utmost loyalty when he must face any community opposition whatsoever. In return, the household head feeds them, clothes them, acts as their protector in local disputes when he can, and helps them with their bridewealth and marriage arrangements. These clients are called *tada njima* (son of the house). They refer to the household head as *abba njima* (father of the house). They treat their *abba njima* with all the discipline and respect that they give their own father and expect from him the same kind of behavior a son expects from a father, indeed more so because only loyalty and obedience, and what one obtains in return for these qualities, can maintain the relationship, since there is no basis in kinship for its continuity.

The important point to be made here is that the Kanuri feel that the *bər-*

zum[3] or discipline-respect ingredients of the father-son relationship can be transferred. This does not mean that they forget their own fathers who are their biological kin. However it does mean that they use the norms of the father-son relationship for self-advancement or for relating to other people as they would to their father, in return for those things that they obtain traditionally from a father. Kanuri were always coming to me and addressing me as their father, or asking for a small gift in the hope that they might repay me with some discipline and respect and begin initiating a *tada njima* role for themselves with me as their *abba njima*. However, there is more to initiating the role than simply asking me for a gift or doing a service. In order for it to work there must be *aman* or trust. A man must know when he brings a client into his household that he will try to behave like a son. Even then he waits patiently and watches to see how firm and fast the professed loyalty really is. Most Kanuri say that a year is not too long a period to wait while testing out the strength of such a relationship before actually giving the person (the *tada njima*) some real responsibilities from which both the household head and the client might gain.

This means of adding to a household can produce very extensive groupings under the proper conditions. If a man has a powerful political post, either in the traditional or modern post-colonial administration, his activities in trade, farming, tax collection, or adjudication means that he can use a large following of loyal and obedient clients. The transferability of the father-son relationship allows men to build up such organizations whenever they have the means to maintain them. Kanuri judge success in life not by wealth or power per se, but by the size of a man's following. And the best indication of this is the size of the household and those related households over which he has some control. Thus great households, the greatest of which is that of the Shehu of Bornu, form the upper class group of Kanuri society. Wealthy traders have many *tada njima* who, after their loyalty has been proven, are given goods and money to go out and trade for their superiors. Bornu society is such that powerful men, indeed any man wishing to raise his status, require loyal followers and clients who use the ingredients of the father-son relationship to define their interpersonal relations. Certainly many of the people a man may depend upon are members of his own descent group, but kinsmen differ from clients in a number of important respects. Kinsmen may profit not only by one another's success, but through inheritance they also gain by each other's death. Or if a particular prerogative, say access to political office of some kind, resides in one male line, then an office-holder's male relatives may profit from his dismissal since one of them may be considered as a replacement. Furthermore relationships based on descent cannot be broken completely—some mutual dependence always remains—even though a superior dislikes the services of his descent group member who is serving as his subordinate. Clientship is more rational in this respect since clients can in effect be "fired" for poor performance of their duties. Thus clientship, represented by the *tada njima* relationship, is a flexible and useful tool in the building of Kanuri households and even larger social groupings.

Finally it is important to remember that all of these important relationships are basically those within a household. This is the stage upon which family life

---

[3] The letter ə is pronounced as the "oo" in "look" or "book."

takes place. Here an individual learns the modes of behavior towards others that he requires for an adequate and successful social life in Kanuri society. The kinship system, the family, and the household produce individuals who can live in other households; and using the basic modes of behavior from household life they can participate in the widely ramified political and economic organization of their society. Thus kinship, family, and household—but most importantly the household and the superior-subordinate relations within it—provide a basis and a locus for maintaining the society and its values in their present form.

4

The Life Cycle: From Birth to Death in Kanuri Society

THE HISTORY of Kanuri society, its family and household organization, and the other groupings described later in this book that make it into a system, are all activated and made real by the people who spend their lives in Bornu. Kanuri society, indeed any society, can be described by giving the major details of its organized social life. However, such a description uses as its units the roles and groups that make up each organization. The units (roles and groups) are separate parts of the system, but it is important to remember that roles and groups are stage settings for the behavior of real people who are born, grow up, love, hate, get married, grow old and die. Some are more successful, some less so, but the way in which they live a Kanuri life from beginning to end is what produces the energy, the continuity, and the change within the structure of their society.

Like people everywhere the Kanuri see a pattern in the life span of individuals. This is thought of as a series of stages or grades determined fundamentally by age and sex. Whether he or she be rich or poor, peasant, slave, or of royal blood these stages still apply and mark off a lifetime. Like age grades in all societies there is a rough correlation at each stage with that of physiological growth, maturation and decline. However, the specific factors of local geography and the adaptation to it, as well as their social complexity and culture history, have molded the grades into the specific set of life stages that can be called Kanuri. In the future, the forces of modernism will add their weight to this stream and produce changes in this traditional cycle. For the present, however, I want to present a picture of a Kanuri lifetime, as my informants report it and as I have observed it in Bornu, starting with gestation and ending with the death of an individual.

Gestation

Kanuri men and women almost universally claim that having children is desirable for married couples, although charms that both promote and prevent pregnancy can be obtained locally from specialists. The culture norms on this point are

53

quite explicit, and married couples are supposed to want children. Those few women who admitted to me, confidentially, not wanting children had very high divorce records, while all others conformed to expectations when asked specifically concerning their desire for offspring.

Traditionally the Kanuri believe that conception results from simultaneous orgasm during sexual intercourse. This information I got from older men who do not, however, know in any detail when or how often such an event actually takes place. Instead they reason that it has occurred when their wife reports a pregnancy. When a woman is over one month late in a menstrual cycle (a few said forty-five days) conception is suspected, and she begins to buy charms on the market to safeguard a normal gestation. During this initial period the husband and wife, ideally at least, should not speak of the pregnancy to anyone until at least the second menstrual period has been missed, and then only to their very close friends and relatives. Such talk, indeed any excess conversation about the pregnancy, is believed to be dangerous to the course and development of a normal pregnancy. Even during the later stages just before birth only very cryptic references are made by the parents when they refer to the coming event. Pregnancy, like a number of other occasions in one's lifetime, is considered a very fragile time, a time when an individual is vulnerable to maliciousness from humans or spirits. Because it is difficult to know about such maliciousness, until after its effects are felt, it is better to avoid mentioning the susceptible circumstances.

Sexual intercourse is continued throughout pregnancy since the Kanuri believe that such activity makes for an easier labor at birth by keeping the passage open and providing fluids for the child and the mother.

Although the Kanuri recognize the pregnancy period of nine months, the woman continues her normal work until the lying-in period is signaled by labor. On the other hand exceptions to the nine-month period occur, and some women claim to have been pregnant for years although no outward sign is visible. This latter condition is referred to as bənji, that is to say an embryo that will not come out of the womb. A woman may miss a menstrual cycle once and then become convinced that she has conceived. If her conviction holds she may, after menstruating again, diagnose the condition as a bənji. Missing a menstrual period, however, is not absolutely necessary for the diagnosis. Women who spoke of having bənji felt that any woman could have one, but they also agreed that in their experience the woman was usually older and either had not given birth for a long time or had had a completely infertile marriage history. Certainly many Kanuri women seem to be barren, and this cultural belief must help to assuage the disappointment of a hopeful but sterile woman. It may also serve to alleviate the loss of womanly role for an older woman who sees herself being replaced in her reproductive functions by her husband's younger wives.

Birth

When the woman is about to give birth, she is assisted by her own mother if she is in the vicinity, or her mother-in-law if she is living with her husband's family, and sometimes by a specialist in midwifery. There are stories told about women who give birth by themselves, but invariably people qualify these remarks by saying that such cases are very rare except for illegitimate births where it is more common for the girl to go off by herself and deliver the baby.

Throughout her confinement and for a short time after the birth, a pregnant woman takes many hot baths which are said to aid her by making her healthy and adding to the health of the baby. Her husband prepares for this by setting aside extra stores of firewood in the compound. At the time of birth the woman sits over a large warmed wooden bowl and delivers in the sitting position. When the infant arrives it is washed, then warmed almost continuously by the women in attendance who heat their hands over a dish of hot coals and then press the body of the child gently. Almost immediately there are attempts to have the child feed at the mother's breast. At the same time the placenta is buried in the compound with no ceremony. If it fails to descend, one of the women in attendance hastens to a local religious practitioner or a medicinal expert who gives medicines to bring it down. All adult men, including the husband, are barred from any direct participation in the birth event. Instead they usually pray during the entire birth along with their friends and a religious practitioner who may have been hired especially for this purpose.

During the forty-day confinement period after the birth the woman remains inside the household, and ideally, there should be no sexual intercourse between the spouses. However, almost everyone agreed that this rule was not strictly followed among the ordinary peasant farmers or craftsmen because of the great reliance played on a woman's labor in the compound and in the fields. On the other hand, the first eight days after the birth are universally accepted as a time of strict confinement. After that, factors of wealth, number of wives, the season of the year, rural or urban residence, and personal idiosyncracy determines the length of confinement for any particular woman.

During the first eight days of its life, the baby is referred to as "the little kitten," or "the little stranger." This is considered a time of great susceptibility for the parents and the new-born infant. The parents are expected to maintain very strict adherence to all cultural prescriptions in order to insure the child's safety. Practically no mention of the new baby is made in public, and even its sex is unknown outside the household except for a few very close friends of the family, and these are expected to keep the secret. "Little kitten" is an appropirate term. Cats are highly thought of in Bornu and are the only animals except peacocks that are believed to have the right to enter heaven. Like a kitten the new baby is a welcome addition to the family; and like a kitten it is not really human. If it dies during these first eight days, it is buried unceremoniously, like a pet, in the women's section of the compound with none of the formal rituals given to a normal member of the community.

On the Friday within the eight-day period or several days before, if the child is born on a Friday, two or three kola nuts are sent around to each of the men of the town who are relatives and friends of the parents. Similar presents are sent to the houses of all the important people in the village—the political, judicial, and religious leaders. On the same day, women who are related to the household by ties of kinship, or common membership in the neighborhood, or long-term friendships gather at the mother's compound and begin to prepare food. Some of this food is given as charity to the older women of the group who have no husbands. Both of these acts, the giving of the food and the sending out of the kola nuts, are said to be the formal announcement of the new baby's birth as well as an invitation to attend the naming ceremony held on the eighth day after birth, that is to say on the same day one week later.

It is worth noting at this point that these precautions are well adapted to the facts of Kanuri life. Infant mortality is extremely common, varying for example between 122 and 240 per thousand in the urban areas where the hospitals have been keeping records. This is especially true of the first few hours and days after birth. One man in Magumeri had only two children alive out of nine born to him and his one wife, and five of these nine had died within the first eight days of life. Although this case is somewhat exceptional, it is not difficult to hear of comparable reports throughout the emirate. The Kanuri see many of these deaths as being the result of someone's or something's (a spirit, for instance) malevolent intentions. Charms and prayers are used and divination by religious leaders is sometimes resorted to because of the insecurity the parents feel over the survival of their new-born infant. Thus the eight-day period before the naming ceremony is a cultural buffer, a cushion that allows for the disappointment and grief associated with the highly possible death of the infant.

The Naming

Early in the morning of the eighth day the formal naming ceremony is performed. As they do for all public gatherings, men and women go separately; the women, in groups formed into single files according to rank, move past the men who are seated on the ground near the entrance to the compound. The ground millet flour and other foods received at this time as gifts allow the wife to prepare her husband's food during her confinement without engaging in a most arduous part of her work—that of grinding the millet into flour. Inside the compound the women sit in front of the mother's hut chatting gaily and coloring their teeth with tobacco flowers and a local plant used specifically for this purpose. The barber and his young assistant or apprentice arrive and cut facemarks on the new-born infant and then remove its uvula. While waiting to carry out this ritual function, the barber and his assistants cut the women's hair free of charge as a mark of the festiveness of the occasion. The women collect some money for the barber which is given to him after the baby has been successfully incised. The ceremony ends when perfume is passed among the women and all assembled dip their fingers in tiny bottles or a glass, then rub the scent over their neck and hands. Many, however, stay on talking and chatting for several hours before drifting back in small groups to their own compounds.

In front of the compound the men sit on mats. On one side of the gate sit the *mallams* (religious practitioners) reading from the Koran. On the other side of the infant's hut are the men of the household sitting in order of seniority with the most senior closest to the door. Next to them are their close friends, relatives, and the highest ranking people in attendance. The rest spread out along the north side of the compound under its front wall and everyone waits for the name to be announced. Every man contributes a small cash gift of two to five shillings, given as a token of friendship and esteem and collected by a close friend of the father of the new child. The money is used to pay the barber and the *mallams* who say prayers to ensure the safety of the child and his future success.

When the barber has finished his work, the father sends in a friend to tell the women the name he has chosen for the new child. Ideally his friend should return and then announce the name to the men outside, but very often the men are told at the same time. Now the baby is a person; it has a name; its sex is known; it has joined the compound and the community. The senior *mallam* leads everyone in a prayer and the ceremony is over. Kola nuts and perfume are passed around among the men and the new father gives a few pennies to each reader of the Koran and several shillings to the senior *mallam*. It is a memorable day for the parents and there is general rejoicing among those who know about the ceremony and are related in some way to the family. One informant put it this way:

> Everyone is happy because the father and mother have shown that they have practiced the customs of our people, and they have shown that they have been blessed with good fortune because "the little kitten" has become a person.

Especially pleased on such occasions is the namesake of the new baby, if he is alive, for it is a public recognition of the respect and affection shown to this person by the family. Very often the name used is that of the grandparent. The Kanuri very often take turns using grandparent's names on both sides of the family although some insist that boys be named from the father's side and girls from the mother's. However, parents may also name children after an important person or a person to whom the father owes some subordination. The Kanuri, like people in many places, avoid using the names of their own parents or parents-in-law and high status or elderly people in general. Therefore the child is given a nickname that often indicates his or her relationship to the person whose name he bears. For example, many Kanuri boys are named Abba Gana (small father) or simply Abba (father) indicating that they have been named after the father of one of their parents. The link to the grandparent is even closer if the latter has been named after *his* grandparent making him a person who is called Abba Gana as well. Thus the grandson can, in practice, share both his grandfather's "real" name and his nickname as well. Sometimes the mother is referred to in a name, or even the order of one's birth in relation to other children. Thus two of the contemporary sons of the royal family in Bornu are called Abba Kiari Kura and Abba Kiari Shuwa. These men are half brothers named after their royal grandfather—Kiari. Indeed Kiari itself is a circumlocution meaning "old" or "the old one." Kura means "the big one" or "the oldest brother," and Shuwa refers to the tribal membership of Abba Kiari Shuwa's mother. Thus one son, Abba Kiari Kura, is called "father, the old one, the eldest," or "the eldest one named after my father, the old one," and the other brother, Abba Kiari Shuwa, is "father, the old one, the Shuwa," or the "son of the Shuwa wife who is named after my father, the old one." Abba Kiari's real name, Mustafa, never appears in these well-known names of his grandsons who are his recognized namesakes. Sometimes a name reflects the title of the person that the child is named after. Thus Mallam Kumbar refers to the title of the particular person's grandfather, who was Kumbar in the court of the king. Or again, sometimes

it refers to a family event, such as Gambo, "the person who was born after twins."
Names, then, reflect many of the social relationships and social circumstances of the
individual being named and his relationship to those around him. However, the
main point of the naming ceremony is quite clear. As one Kanuri put it,

> We celebrate the naming because the child and the family are fortunate; the
> infant has escaped death and entered successfully into life; it is therefore a joyful
> occasion.

Infancy

For the first eighteen months of his life a child is referred to exclusively as
tiful or new-born infant without anyone referring to its age. The period marks the
beginning of the infant's membership in society and its most obvious sign is breast-
feeding. Perhaps the best single word to describe the infant period is that of "introduction," for during these first few months the baby is introduced to the family,
to friends of the family, the neighborhood, the ward, indeed to the community as a
whole.

Any jealousy or antagonism felt towards the new baby by its older brothers
and sisters is recognized as such and dealt with firmly but gently. Even cats are
supposed to be jealous of new babies and are prevented by adults from coming
near them. Very often an older brother or sister is sent away from the house to a
nearby compound during the period of the birth, especially if there is a grandparent living close by. On the day of the naming ceremony all the older children in
the family up to the age of ten receive little gifts in honor of the occasion. At one
ceremony we saw a little boy of two and a half being brought back from the
grandparent's house where he had been living for about a week. He was brought to
the new infant and told, "This is our new baby. Be kind to him and look after
him." All the children of the household were given little gifts that same day and
told the same thing. After the ceremony was over many of the women in the compound devoted some time to playing with the children and showing them affection.
Everyone pointed out repeatedly what a fine thing it was for the children to have a
new brother in the family. If during the next few weeks the older children should
show any signs of hostility they are sent away again to another compound for periods up to a month or two. At this new compound they are told again and again
about the necessity of showing affection and being responsible for younger brothers
and sisters. In other words, "sibling rivalry" is understood, anticipated, and dealt
with in a way that reduces tensions and calmly recognizes the normality of an older
child's jealousy when all attention turns to a new baby in the family.

The new infant spends most of its first eighteen months with its mother.
However, short sorties with older sisters occur now and then. On the other hand,
the father has very little to do with the child at this stage, although he often comes
by to see it. The baby soon learns to sit quietly while it is swaddled in a straddling-
sitting position on its mother's back. Toilet training at this stage is minimal. The
mother, rather than the child, tries to learn when the child is likely to urinate. At
first the child is merely wiped clean by the mother, but as soon as it can sit up, it is
placed astride her ankles with its back resting on her upturned feet. A little hole is

dug in the sandy soil between the ankles and the infant then has a simple and comforting toilet ready made for it by the mother. Afterwards its loins are washed and the hole covered up with sand. During the entire infant stage breast-feeding is carried on easily and simply upon demand by the infant for the breast. Indeed the breast is generally used as a pacifier.

A typical scene in a mother's hut illustrates the way in which the introduction of a new baby to society is carried out. The mother and her friends sit around chatting and they pass the baby around, dandling it in turn, although the baby remains with the mother for a large part of the time. A very common topic of conversation at such times is, quite unsurprisingly, the new baby. But unlike a similar group of American ladies most of the talk is *to* and not *about* the baby. The mother and many of those present tell the uncomprehending infant in sing-song voices about its kindred, "So-and-so is your father, so-and-so is your brother, so-and-so is your sister," and so on through a vast complex of kinship links on both the mother's and the father's side of the family. The infant is also told in the same way about its neighborhood, its section of the town, or its village, its political leaders, and so on. "So-and-so is your village head, so-and-so is your district head, and this is your tribe and this is your emirate, and this is your *Shehu,* and so-and-so is your Waziri." The family occupation is also mentioned and how soon the infant is going to help in such-and-such activities around the compound and grow up into successful adulthood within the framework of all the associations and expectations that are referred to constantly.

Why tell a baby about its social connections, occupational expectations, political affiliations, and so on? Certainly later on, when it can understand a little more of the language, such talk is a means of initiating it into the social groupings of the society. However at this stage another function is performed. The child is a new member of the society, and it is being introduced into and given a recognizable place in its social setting. The new member means new relationships. So-and-so who did not have a younger brother's son, now has one; someone else now has a new cousin and perhaps a future spouse; or someone else now has a sister's son or an additional one. The coming of the *tiful* or infant creates changes because a new member has been added and in introducing it to society people are asked to shift their understanding of the organizations which now must include this new member. By constantly referring to these new relationships during the infant's first few months people close to the family affirm to themselves and finally to others the fact that many relationships are different now that the new baby has arrived safely.

As far as training goes, the *tiful* is too young to be very harshly dealt with or to be told not to do this or that. Its primary task is to survive and grow into a useful, law-abiding, member of its community.

Childhood

Infancy ends as weaning begins, about the end of the eighteenth month although a good deal of variation exists in actual practice so that many are weaned earlier. In general weaning is carried out with a matter-of-fact attitude as if to say,

"This is just a common, everyday matter," and should not be thought of as giving anyone any trouble. When difficulties do arise an older woman of the compound or the family offers her breast as a pacifier. In the odd case where this does not succeed pressures tighten up. The breast is referred to as "dirty" or specifically as "excreta" and in extreme instances bitter grounds of leaves are put on the breast and the lesson is very quickly learned.

After weaning, pressures are slowly brought to bear to teach the child proper ways of living among its people. Thus, as soon as a child can totter, the adult woman in whose hut he is sleeping starts to enforce the rule that he or she should go outside to perform toilet functions, stoop over with knees bent and buttocks near the ground using only the left hand for any attentions necessary to elimination. Later on as language skills develop the importance of the left hand is more highly emphasized as well as the advisability of being discreet about toilet functions. After the age of two and a half or three, scolding gets more intense and the child is told it is dirty or bad for urinating on the floor. Naturally the severity of the training depends to a large extent as well on the particular situation, the mood and personality of the mother, or other socializing agents present, as well as the age of the child. Thus a grandmother was observed who was not overly excited when her two-year-old grandson urinated on the floor, but she became quite angry when he wet her bed.

Patient but continuous teaching by adults in the household is a constant part of everyday activities for the young child. The following excerpt from field notes tells its own story:

> A plate of food is on the floor of the hut gathering flies. The grandmother says to her little grandson, "Kachella, pick up the plate. Now, take it over there. Be careful, there is food on the plate. Now, take that other plate and cover the food over. (Plates are made of grass.) That's right, very good." This simple operation which would have taken the grandmother a few seconds has been carried out after two patient minutes of instruction to the child who could not yet speak more than a few words.

Childhood also ushers in the establishment of sex roles. Boys are now called "small boys" and girls are "small girls" or "three heads" referring to the three-pronged hair style of prepubescent girls. Boys and girls wear different clothes and begin fairly soon to associate with members of their own sex and to carry out chores that are specifically for boys or for girls. In play groups based on sex they wander freely about the village or neighborhood of the city gathering like flies to honey at the slightest hint of any excitement, and wandering further afield from their own compound as they get older. The girl comes quickly under the authority of the women of the household especially her own mother if she is brought up at home. She learns the intricacies of preparing food, carrying water, and the ever-present task of grinding millet either at a quern or by pounding it on a large wooden mortar. The boys begin to gather firewood, help with the farming, run messages, gather grass for a horse if there is one, tend the goats and sheep of the compound, and learn the family dry-season occupation. Pressure to learn these skills is slow but definite. Punishments are rare, but severe. The child is beaten with a rod or whip until neighbors and friends succeed in persuading the parents to cease or desist. Reasons given for the beating often concern the sudden, or continual dereliction of some duty although outright malfeasance such as stealing can also bring swift and awesome retribution. For example, a young boy was beaten for continually omitting to gather grass for his father's horse. This is a skill that a boy should acquire by the age of six or eight, possibly nine at the very latest. When punishment occurs its severity is noted by all children within earshot, and thus the beating of one child of the village or ward serves notice on all that punishment is not just a matter of threats but may become a reality if limits are transgressed.

That such household learning soon becomes habitual can be seen any day in a Bornu village by watching children. Even a little girl of three and a half can accomplish tasks involving quite a lot of dexterity. One little girl of this age was passed a straw mat plate and separately given some paper clips. She neatly put the paper clips on the plate and began her own already advanced imitation of the quick, deft, jiggling movements associated with the sifting of ground-nut shells. None of her paper clips was dropped, and she soon passed the plate back saying, "Here are some sifted ground nuts."

Sometimes play takes in both sexes and is more complex than simple imitation like the one above. Thus for several days a large group of young children from the age of five through ten may organize a "wedding." The "bride" and "groom" are chosen as are the various kindred, the best man, the leading woman, etc. Care is taken to practice as many of the details of the adult virgin wedding ceremony as they can manage including even a mock impregnation, in this case with a small doll. Wedding foods in miniature are passed around to the adults who accept the mock food with a show of seriousness although they may comment on or question some detail of the ceremony carried out mistakenly or omitted by the children. Adults expressed satisfaction with this type of play and remarked on its instructive value for the children. Such play is related to an even more complex form called *mai-mai,* which is no longer practiced in Bornu. In playing *mai-mai* the young children in a village put on a pageant. They chose a king, nobles, servants, slaves, wives, gave titles to everyone, and behaved for several days in the guise of these socio-political roles. Mock battles were fought, slaves taken and justice meted out in a mock court. Seniority was established by age and consent. The organization was temporary like the "wedding" and disbanded after a few days. During periods when adults are out of the compound, away at a market, or working in the fields during the growing season, children often play house. The group gets together and appoints "fathers," "wives," and "children." The little children may actually cook for their "husbands" on such occasions and the couples go into a hut in the compound where sexual play is carried on. They are, however, soon called back to the larger group where it has been declared "morning" by another child who has announced the "morning prayers" signifying that night has passed. Boys are aware that such play should stop when they can ejaculate. From then on they are men; sex is a serious affair and unmarried girls are illegitimate objects of sexual intercourse. However such prepubescent sex derived from playing "house" is widespread, or to paraphrase one young informant, "Everyone does such things when they are young."

Boys especially, but girls as well, may also begin some religious instruction during their childhood. Although girls never leave home for this purpose, boys sometimes do after the age of six or seven. In some cases the teacher lives nearby and the boys go there to learn their prayers and the beginning of Islamic theology. In some cases, especially with girls, the instruction is taken in the household itself. During adolescence this training may become more serious, and boys who were not sent to live with their religious teachers before may go off to learn Islamic practices in greater detail. The relationship of a boy to his *mallam* or religious teacher is expressed in the saying, "Your mallam exceeds your father." In other words, a boy's religious instructor exceeds his father in fatherly qualities and he must be respected and obeyed as a superior whose authority is unquestioned.

Whether a child goes to live with his religious teacher or not, there are other important factors that maintain for him a high turn-over among household members that is in striking contrast to the norms of western society. No matter where he lives in Bornu there is a high divorce rate and the possibility that his mother and father will not live together all their lives is very great indeed. Children stay under the control of their father in his household, although some contact with the mother is maintained and remains a strong emotional bond for many, even though there is a constant possibility that it cannot remain a household relationship. High divorce also means that the mother's co-wives are continually changing and that one's own half-siblings may be without their own mother in the compound so that compound relationships themselves are continually shifting and changing throughout a person's childhood.

The Kanuri also practice fostering. In some cases children are given to grandparents, or friends, or other relatives to be raised. Sometimes the reasons are political, and the parents try to place the child in a very important person's household so that the child may grow up knowing and associating with people who can help him later on in life. Sometimes it is felt to be a kindness towards a friend or to the child's grandparents. Whatever the reason, the child lives during his early years in a compound other than that of his own parents. It is possible to find Kanuri who have lived in as many as four or five compounds by the time they reach adolescence, and two or three is quite common. On the other hand, there are also many people—especially in rural areas where their work is needed—who were raised in only one household. One informant reported how he was given to a father's younger brother at weaning, given to a religious teacher at six, returned to his father at the age of eight, then put into the household of the district head when he was thirteen. Although there is much variation in this practice, in conjunction with the high divorce rate as well as the always present possibility of sudden death by disease, it means again that the actual people in the younger person's relational network are many, many, times more fluid and changing than is the case in western society.

Summing up this very important point, we may say that it is a rare Kanuri who has passed through childhood with a stable set of interpersonal relations to siblings or adult members of his household. This means that in child training the relationships to specific persons are not stressed as much as the norms of behavior we spoke of in Chapter 3. The one important exception to this is the relationship to one's mother which is particularly strong between a mother and her son. This fits nicely into the life cycle of women who, as we shall see, usually return to their son later in their old age to take up the role of old, unmarried women. In stressing the norms of behavior rather than particular relationships, it is respect and obedience to seniors, first in the household then in the society at large, that is the most important social learning of childhood. Kanuri society is hierarchical. Whether the person is in one compound or another, one social situation or another, there is always one common feature—rank and its determinants, power and authority. By living in several compounds, by seeing authority at work in the community, and by learning to generalize his response to authority, the young child learns to respond easily and gracefully to many combinations of rank and position. His counterpart in western society may be learning how to cope with the intricacies of modern urban technology, but he would certainly be no match for his Kanuri counterpart in the diplomacy necessary in dealing with superiors.

Puberty

Puberty is not an age-grade in the same sense as childhood or adolesence. Yet it deserves some special attention because it is a marker that separates these two life periods and creates a means for very important transitions especially for young girls. Sometime between the age of twelve and fourteen most girls undergo their first marriage. Boys on the other hand begin their adolescence. This is a more carefree time for them than the period of intense training for adulthood that a girl is suddenly confronted with as she moves from childhood into her teenage period and marriage.

However there are no absolutely sharp breaks even for a girl. A newly married young girl is not considered totally grown-up and sometimes she continues to wear her hair in the childhood style. If she divorces during this early period, usually the first three or four years after her first marriage, people often speak of her as *njim suri* or one who is only beginning to become a woman but who has not completed the change-over to full adultlhood.[1] At first the young wife still sees many unmarried childhood friends who will soon be getting married themselves. They visit her when she is confined to the house for varying periods depending upon how secluded her husband wishes his wife to be. Only gradually over the period of the first year or so of marriage does the young girl begin to participate fully as a wife. From the first she cooks food regularly because it is her duty and her right, and as time goes on she is seen more and more in the company of the older, adult women of the compound and the neighborhood. If she is not in total seclusion, like most rural wives, then she can be seen going with the women to the well or the market, and to women's festivities in the village.

Although rare it sometimes happens that a girl misses the opportunity to marry while still in her early teens. Leaving aside the very few girls who go on in school, such cases are rather tragic. The girl is either mentally deficient or a disturbed person, or one who people say has been having love affairs before marriage. In such cases she changes her hair style in her middle to late teens and takes on the role of a single divorced woman seeking a new husband and therefore open to courtship and sexual liaisons with men.

In Magumeri one young girl about fifteen or sixteen who was well de-

---

[1] Literally *njim suri* means to have seen inside the hut, that is she has been alone with her husband but only seen or glimpsed at the activities of adulthood not really practiced them in full.

veloped physically had not yet married. There were many rumors and much gossip to the effect that she was no longer a virgin and that men of the town slept with her. Her father, it was said, would have a hard time arranging her first marriage. The girl herself seemed to be suffering increasingly from her inability to see herself in the role of a child awaiting marriage instead of that of a developing young matron—the role now common among her young age mates. Thus in order to take up a normal position in society, girls are supposed to have their first marriages in and around the time of puberty. Failure to do so indicates a deviant and degrading development. This is the reason why almost all Bornu men say that girls who go on in the educational system are "spoiled" and should never be allowed to stay in school beyond the traditional age of marriage. The girls in school see the matter differently; the situation remains today one of tension, with the majority against education for girls, and the schools themselves looking for students and preaching a somewhat different attitude toward a girl's adolescence than that held traditionally by the people.

Another point should also be noted. Most girls have very little choice, if any, in their first marriage arrangements. If they are very drastically opposed to the union, their views are considered since parents are afraid they might behave badly as young wives. However they are traditionally supposed to respect the wishes of their parents and comply with their demands. Indeed many Kanuri, both men and women, know very little about their first marriage arrangements at all since these are almost entirely made by their parents or the head of the compound they are living in at the time. It should also be realized that many Kanuri girls marry for the first time with men sometimes as much as two, three, and even four times their own age which enhances the traditional seniority of the husband as well as taking any "romance" out of it for the girls.

Sometime around the end of childhood and into the beginning of the teen-age period young boys are circumcized. This event is fundamentally a ceremonial occasion and is thus related only in a rough general way to the actual onset of puberty for each boy. Generally speaking boys are cut in groups, although in rural areas it is not uncommon to see a family performing the ceremony for just one boy in the household. On the other hand circumcision among high-ranking people such as village heads, district heads, members of the royal family, or rich traders in the city attracts many other families who try to have their own children cut at the same time to participate in the large festivities. Usually the higher the rank of the leading families involved in a circumcision the greater the number of boys who are likely to be cut at the same time.

The important thing is not the readiness of the boy. Rather it is the auspiciousness of the occasion in terms of the family's relationship to the rest of the community. Is there a large circumcision taking place this year? Are a large number of friends and relatives asking when little Abba Gana is going to be circumcized? Have the household members, especially the household head, attended a great many marriage or naming ceremonies? Have other community members been given gifts on these occasions? Is it not time to reap the benefit of all this participation by having a ceremony of one's own to which many people will come and bring gifts of food, clothing, and money for the family and the boy? These and similar questions are the determining factors in the timing of the circumcision ceremony, and they point to the major functions of the event. Certainly it marks publicly the opening of the gates on the road to manhood for the young man, but, much more importantly, it validates, strengthens and dramatizes the relational network of ties that the family and the household maintain and attempt to promote in the society.

At some of the larger ceremonies, especially those held by the high-ranking households in Bornu, there is often a small group of recent converts who ask to join the ceremony in order to mark their religious conversion and obtain full membership in Kanuri society. In one very large circumcision we saw forty-seven boys from high status households and ten Cameroon pagans ranging in age from fifteen to thirty-five. These latter seemed completely ecstatic to have been accepted at the ceremony and were the subject of much ribald joking by the Kanuri participants. However they now had an easier access to Kanuri women as wives and sweethearts, and it is conceivable that when they do in fact marry Kanuri women they and their descendants will eventually be absorbed into Kanuri society. Thus the circumcision ceremony is one of the important gateways into society for non-Moslems from the small tribes surrounding Bornu on its southern and southeastern borders.

As in many cultures around the world, the Kanuri themselves regard the circumcision ceremony as a mark of approaching manhood, and even though the boys are often quite young the ceremony still dramatizes their adult or approaching adult status. Thus after the boys have come out of confinement during which the cut heals, they are given whips which they brandish while chasing and threatening the young girls. The girls must "buy off" such treatment by giving the young boy a few pennies. This ritual was left unexplained by informants who answered questions about its meaning by saying, "We do this because it is our custom." However, it seems likely that it is a symbolic reference to the achievement of manhood or potential manhood. It symbolizes through ritual the cultural value of male dominance which the boys must now begin to practice as they prepare to join the ranks of adult men. The "buying off" of the beating by the little girls can be interpreted to reflect the flexibility of female submissiveness; a woman must behave submissively towards a man but she has levers to gain her own rights and wishes in her relationships with men.

Adolescence

As we have seen, there is an extra age-grade period for boys which lasts from around the time of circumcision to their first marriage between the ages of eighteen and twenty-five. At first the young man is still thought of as a small boy, but as he advances into middle and late teenage years he becomes more of a *zairo*— that is to say, a young bachelor. He associates in his free time with other young men his age and begins to gossip about trade, politics, and nocturnal adventures with women. Young boys generally obtain their first sexual experience in their mid to late teenage period from divorced women who are often older than themselves. In their later teens and early twenties they begin to have more serious love affairs of longer duration with young divorced women who may turn out to be their future wives if their first marriages are not already arranged by their parents.

Sitting and listening to a group of these young men discussing matters of interest one is struck by the similarities and the differences in their lives as compared to similar groups in western society. Like young men everywhere they discussed the merits of various occupations, the economic returns, the power and prestige to be gained from one or the other type of job, and so on. Unlike their counterparts in western society, they also spend a great deal of time discussing the qualities of "the big men" in Bornu and the benefits received by loyal followers of these men. They are keenly aware, or try to be, of whose fortunes are rising and falling among the big men and listen with great interest to some new tidbit of information to this effect. Like their counterparts elsewhere teenagers learn to smoke cigarettes, gamble, and drink alcoholic beverages during this period. School boys also learn western table manners and take periodic meals in the places that serve western style food.

One of the most important features of a Kanuri boy's adolescence is his choice of training for an occupation. All young boys learn the fundamentals of farming in the households of their youth since almost all compound heads in Bornu, except some in the city, have farms. In some rural villages boys will learn nothing else but farming and probably remain farmers all their lives. On the other hand the majority of Kanuri boys learn another occupation which they will practice during the dry season or the non-farming season. For most boys the choice is determined ahead of time by the elders of the household, or by the economic specializations in their own vicinity. For example, one boy whose father is a salt retailer and who lives with his father in the ward of the dyers has been apprenticed by his father to one of the dyer households. In general boys are expected to take up the occupation of their fathers unless they or their parents have strong desires and an opportunity to do something else. There is much evidence to show that in making the decision the wishes of the young boys were taken into account. Thus one young man remarked that he would never comply with his father's desire that he become a butcher. Instead he started to work with his father's younger brother in the nearby compound and is learning to be a trader in hides and skins. Today a large range of new occupations is opening up; modernization has served to accelerate this degree of freedom simply because there are many more occupations and a wider range of potential income.

Kanuri occupations other than farming usually involve some apprenticeship, especially for young boys. Such training varies with the kind of job being learned, with the age of the boy, and with the nature of the relationship between the boy and the man teaching him the occupation. If an occupation has a higher status or there is an expectation of high income or prestige associated with it, the person doing an apprenticeship must expect a longer training period in return for having been admitted into an advantageous position. Thus truck drivers who make a comparatively high income demand a fee besides three to five years of service from the person taken on as an apprentice. Butchers occupy a low-status position in the society, but they can also earn fairly good incomes and therefore they, too, claim longer than usual apprenticeship. As the boy becomes older, it is expected that his training period will become shorter, whereas the earlier an apprenticeship is begun, the longer the education. This simply reflects Kanuri recognition of the more rapid learning that comes with age.

The terms of the relationship are dictated by the boy and his immediate family or compound head, on the one hand, and the master instructor on the other. If there is a recognized kinship link between the boy and his future teacher and the compound head, then arrangements are much looser than if this is not the case. In the latter situation there is generally hard bargaining over the terms of the relationship. In general the boy must live in the master's house for a stipulated period helping with all the work of the household, the farming, bringing grass for the horse if there is one, running messages, and helping in the occupational specialization of his master. He is a *tada njima,* or son of the house, and refers to his new household head as *abba njima,* or father of the house. He is supposed to act in the situation in the same way as a son acts towards his father. If the master is already a relative, he refers to the apprentice by the appropriate kin term in the manner laid out for such relationships within the culture, although he has added authority in this particular situation. Arrangements in such cases are often made early in the boy's life and last longer, coming closer in effect to a true adoption. A number of men reported having difficulty ending such relationships when they wish to go out on their own, especially when the master is also related by kinship to the apprentice. On the other hand, all Kanuri accept subordination as the means to valued ends. The following case will give some idea of the details involved in such a relationship.

A young barber apprentice of about nineteen or twenty years of age had previously been apprenticed to a seller of kola nuts. However he decided to give it up because it entailed the constant giving of credit to his customers and he never seemed able to collect all the money owed to him. His full brother in Maiduguri who had been his wholesale supplier advised him to return to their home town and become a barber. The older brother claimed that it was a good occupation and furthermore one of the barbers back in Magumeri needed an apprentice since his own son was as yet too young to help in the work. The young boy returned to Magumeri to ask the barber about it and then completed his own arrangements for the apprenticeship. He moved into the barber's compound for one year and became his apprentice. He could visit the compound in which his mother lived and attend his own farm plots. But he had to cultivate the barber's land, gather grass for the horse, carry water now and then, and be ready at all times to run messages for his *abba njima.* The barber taught him how to shave heads and cup blood (for medicinal purposes), and gave him a barber's bag of tools with which he began working sometimes with his master, sometimes alone.[2] By rights all the proceeds earned during that year were supposed to be given to the master barber. Naturally he pocketed an occasional fee but not too often; to do so would have been to risk his mentor's dissatisfaction and also his projected career as a barber. The senior could, had he felt the boy to be completely unsatisfactory, dismiss him and take back the barber's tools. The barber clothed and fed him and gave him a little spending money regularly during that first year. At special events such as naming ceremonies he was given a small tip by the household head because of his role as the barber's apprentice. This he kept for himself. In 1957 he moved into the compound occupied by his mother in Magumeri. He still considers himself a *tada njima* of the

---

[2] Like many peoples of West Africa, the wider Islamic world, and even Europe not so long ago, the Kanuri believe that taking out a little blood can rid a person of various ailments. They do this by making a few shallow incisions, then sucking the blood into a cattle horn.

barber and still carries out special chores for his former master. He also claims that he gives the senior barber about fifty percent of all his present receipts. As yet he does not know how to cut face marks, remove the uvula, or perform circumcisions, and so he attends all of these ceremonies with the master barber so that he may continue his education. He hopes that by the next year he will be allowed to perform some of these more advanced operations under supervision. When he has completely finished his education, it will not be necessary to do any chores for the senior or give him any commission. Nevertheless the former apprentice should always pay his respects to his ex-master and give him gifts from time to time.

Other apprentices living with strangers claimed they felt more freedom in the household of the stranger and thus live away from home for their training even though they practice the same craft as their father. Many said that they would return home eventually but for the present it was pleasant to travel around seeing other parts of Bornu. This freedom refers more specifically to their sexual activity or at least to its discussion since the discipline and respect given to the compound head is the same as elsewhere. However many boys discussed sex in front of the compound head while such behavior would be impossible in their natal family households. Some boys reported that their father was dead and they had been sent off by their families to the household of relatives or friends in order to learn an occupation.

In summary, adolsecence sharply divides men and women. A young girl takes on her role as a married woman and it is within marriage that she completes her education for adulthood in Kanuri society. A woman may divorce later on as indeed most do, then remarry and bear children throughout. However the framework of adult life is entered into at a first marriage sometime around puberty. For the boy, on the other hand, adolescence is a socially recognized state in life entered at circumcision. This stage of life is used to complete the young man's education and equip him with the interpersonal and occupational skills that are required as an adult and a potential family head.

Maturity

The mature man is described by the Kanuri as *rashidi*. Ideally this implies that he is married, has a compound of his own and an occupation, the use of some land for farming, and a recognized position in the community as the head of a compound. It also means that he has a certain degree of independence so that if he wished he could move of his own accord to another community. To be a mature man par excellence, he should also have children and the reputation of a person who does things discreetly and diplomatically. Maturity is not simply a term applied to a period of life. It is also a value judgement describing a proper and desirable behavior of an adult man. It is not just a role but an evaluation of that role.

Most people seemed unable or unwilling to answer the question of age in relation to maturity, and so they fell back on marriage claiming that any married man was in fact a mature adult. However a few, notably high ranking people, did give an age and suggested that a person could not be thought of as being fully mature until he was at least thirty-five, very often forty. After this age he is not supposed to divorce so often; he is not supposed to have liaisons with divorced women, and he is supposed to behave in a judicious manner as one of the leading members of his community. Thus many young married men living in or near the compound of an older relative or some non-relative, who might be a political and economic superior, refused to be called mature even when they were married. They claimed that they were still young men and that they had still some way to go before they could be called mature adults. Carrying this point further, men whose occupation required that they remain in close subordinate relationship to a superior for most of their lives limited the application of the word "mature" to themselves, and did so rather proudly. For example, one man of about forty-five, whose father had been a servant of the district head's father and who was himself a lifelong servant of the district head of Magumeri, accepted a definition of himself in general as a mature man. Indeed he said, laughingly, he would soon be an old man. He explained that he was mature because he had a married daughter, a farm, a nice compound, a wife who he asserted proudly had stayed with him for eight years, and for all these reasons he thought he should be dubbed "mature." When asked in the same context if he would ever go to live somewhere independently of his district head without the latter's instructions, he quickly replied, "Oh no! In that sense, I am still a small boy." This was in no way shameful for him since his recognition in the community and his status in the society as a whole stands upon his subordinate relationship to the district head.

There is no similar status term among women comparable to the male term for the mature man whose meaning also embodies the same ideology of adult behavior. The woman who has had a child can be referred to by a special term that indicates that she has achieved the important goal of motherhood and added a new member to her husband's household and to both of their families. Middle-aged women can be referred to by another term which distinguishes them from younger woman and from old women whether or not they have given birth to children. In practice such terms are not observed in common use, the woman's status and age being described in other terms.

Ideally an adult woman should be married and should desire to remain so. She should be obedient to her husband, have and want children, and perform her womanly tasks promptly and efficiently while remaining chaste within the walls of her husband's compound, leaving it only when absolutely necessary. She should, however, maintain contact with her own family and return there for important family ceremonies. As one would expect, those who come closest to this ideal in their own behavior often tend to agree with this image of womanly perfection and give it their unqualified support. However those who divorce often and easily tend to qualify their agreement. Thus in answer to the question, "What would you do if your husband demanded you always stay inside the compound?" a woman who had been married to the same man for twenty-five years answered simply, "He is the head of the household," meaning "I must obey." Contrarily, a woman who at the age of thirty-five had been married and divorced four times replied, "Then I would make him divorce me. I would leave him immediately."

While men who are unmarried or between marriages live very similar lives to married men, divorced women are striking in their contrast to their married sisters. A married woman among the Kanuri is tied to her husband's household and must ask his permission to do anything. To be seen speaking to another man is grounds for divorce. On the other hand a divorced woman is free. She comes and goes as she pleases and speaks to whoever she pleases quite freely. Some women quite frankly remark that they prefer this status to that of marriage while others just as strongly remark that they would like to get a husband.

In summary, maturity is a time of achievement for men in which they become full-fledged members of their community. They marry, try to raise families, and become heads of successful and productive households. Women try to marry successfully and hopefully to have children. However, as I have pointed out elsewhere, tensions caused by the demands of subordination in their married role produce strains and rebelliousness that very often leads to the break-up of marriage.[3] In the final analysis the culture is androcentric; there are many means by which men can become successful—through their occupation, their associations with neighbors, relatives, friends, and important men, and through membership and finally headship of a household. In spite of a turnover in wives associated with the high amount of divorce, the household itself is a stable unit, although its personnel is not. On the other hand, it is the rare Kanuri woman who can achieve a successful adulthood. Many women are barren or have had children who have not survived. Very few women remain married to the same men all their lives and most have had one or more extended periods of being divorced and looking for a husband. By centering on men and emphasizing their needs and wishes, Kanuri culture has produced a strain on women that is a fertile field for changes when modernization produces the possibility of new goals for women and new means for achieving them.

Old Age

Old age is signalled in both sexes by the whitening of body hair even though other body characteristics may remain strong and healthy. For both old men and women this last period in life means that many of the obligations and responsibilities of adult life are slowly relinquished, although men generally feel that they belong to the adult roles much longer than women. As heads of households and office holders in governmental positions, men wield powers in a number of spheres and give these up slowly and reluctantly as old age drains away their energy and efficiency. Ideally in Kanuri culture a man should reach the golden years of his life in his old age. If all goes well he receives much respect; his work is carried on by descendants, and his position as a household head may have grown to the point where he is the senior authority among a group of households organized along the lines of a patrilocal extended family with clients, sons, brothers, and their wives and families looking to him for leadership. When he is very old and becoming progressively infirm, he lets many of these duties pass to mature members of the group. Even then they always consult him on decisions and pay heed to his wishes.

The reality in Kanuri society is often far from the ideal although the ideal is a very widely agreed upon goal. To obtain this most desirable position in old age a

[3] See Ronald Cohen, "Marriage instability among the Kanuri of Northern Nigeria," *American Anthropologist*, Vol. 63, 1231–1249.

man must have had a very successful life and belong to the upper ranks of society where power and wealth give him the opportunity to build up the necessary following during his lifetime. Peasants can achieve the ideal if they have through accident or a successful career been able to build up political and economic resources that enable them to maintain a growing compound. For those men who cannot obtain a position of semi-independent leadership in their old age, there is also the possibility of membership in someone else's organization. In this way a man can look forward to a secure position even though his own household as part of it is a very small one. For many other men old age brings neither leadership nor successful subordination. A son, friend, or neighbor may regularly help with the farm plot, or if less successful the man and perhaps an aging wife live alone in a small compound in their village. He is given some general respect as an older person. If he lives in the same community as his children there may be young grandchildren constantly around, and whether they live in the same community or not he may be fostering one of more grandchildren in his compound. Whatever the alternative, and unlike our own society, old age even at its poorest provides an accepted and respected place for old men.

Many old women after a number of divorces or the death of a husband with whom they have lived for many years do not or cannot marry again. This does not seem to be the case nearly so often for the men. If the woman has a son, he is expected to keep her in his compound which may have been the compound of her husband. If she has no son, she may stay in or near the compound of some other relative, including an ex-husband whom she refers to by using the kin term applied to "brother."[4] I have seen a few old women living alone in the compound of their dead husbands although, like old men, most of these seemed in constant touch with young children. Whether or not she is being supported economically by her relatives, any old woman in the lower ranks of society has an accepted role as a small retail seller who sits daily in front of the compound or small market stalls around the town, or near a well, selling a few ground-nuts, sundries, cooked food, or tobacco flowers for staining the teeth of women. Four old women in Magumeri, one of whom lived completely alone, had saved up money to buy themselves a native well, and these four supported themselves on a fairly steady income from the sale of the water. Such practices are not suddenly started; a woman raises extra cash throughout her entire life by petty trade or the sale of cooked foods and with the onset of old age she merely extends these activities into a full-time occupation.

Women from higher ranking households remain in the compounds of their sons or relatives. Very likely they have been secluded as young married women and this continues in their old age. The widow of a high-ranking man is on occasion supported in his compound by the heir to the household. However, if the new household head has his own aging mother alive, then it is more common for the widow to leave her dead husband's household and return to her own kin since her co-wife is now taking over the position of mother of the head of the household. Many of these upper class women have more capital than their lower class counterparts. This started with their dowry and may have been increased through inheritance and trade since the time of their youth. Such trade is carried

---

[4] The Kanuri use a single kin term to refer to brother, sister, cousins of any kind, and half brothers and sisters, although each of these can be distinguished if need be.

on by intermediaries because of the seclusion common among upper class women. If the activity has proven successful during their life it is carried on into old age, and if not then it is dropped. Thus old women, like men, in Bornu have a place in society. It is not generally a position of great authority, although there are some notable exceptions. Certainly, however, deference and respect for the aged is a universal feature of good Kanuri manners. Blessing the young is a cultural symbol of this respect. Old people bless young people when the latter go on trips or there is some special event such as a birth or the naming of a new baby. The seriousness with which such blessings are given and received is evidence of the importance placed on the special capacities of wisdom and propriety that the Kanuri associate with old age.

Death

Just as pregnancy marks the potential beginning of life, so death marks the end. The Kanuri have a quiet accepting attitude toward death; it is unpleasant, but it is always there. The high mortality rate for children, and the desirability that as many as possible in a community attend a funeral means that Kanuri adults attend many more of these ceremonies than people in western society. Thus death and funerals are much more commonly noted and accepted than in the United States where the entire subject is considered repugnant.

The Kanuri believe that going to funerals helps the deceased person to achieve paradise. The more prayers said by as many people as possible and as many religious leaders as possible, then the better are the chances of success. Indeed this is not only true in death but throughout life. People go to a particular funeral because the deceased was "a man of our town," or they attend one in another locality because the person was a relative or a friend. Not to go, even to the funeral of a very low status person of one's own village, is unthinkable. A high ranking official of Magumeri remarked at a funeral of a poor, very old, butcher that only twenty years ago he would not have shaken the hand of such a man, but times have changed. However, when asked whether he would have attended such a man's funeral in former times he looked incredulous; there could be no question about it if they were of the same community. Thus death ties a community together and expresses one's membership in it. No matter what other differences may exist between people, there is one occasion when the only criterion for active participation is a common residence in the same locality.

The compulsion to go to funerals is very strong. Thus a young woman who teaches in the Bornu secondary school system and is highly westernized in many of her attitudes told me that she had to go to a funeral about 100 miles away in the bush. This involved very uncomfortable travel by lorry, then a long horseback ride in the rainy season. However, she never once considered the possibility that she might not attend even though there was every likelihood she would miss the ceremony. Her relatives were having a funeral—therefore she must go; there was no choice although she preferred not to go.

Kanuri burial ceremonies themselves are held as close to the first morning after death as is possible. I observed only one exception to this rule; a very old man in Magumeri died in the morning and was buried in the afternoon. The people explained this by saying that it was the hot season and he had died early in the morning. To wait until the next morning, they said, was too long and not good for the community. This was an oblique way of referring to the belief that the ghost of a dead man is dangerous especially to children until he is buried.

The ceremony itself is quite simple. The body is washed, wrapped in a white cloth and placed on a bier, and then taken out to the burial grounds by the men. Prayers are said continually and the family mourns officially for forty days by saying special prayers and remaining close to home. During the ceremony men remain impassive, quietly telling their beads and praying softly to themselves. Women, on the other hand, come in groups walking slowly in single file wailing and crying, especially if the deceased is a close neighbor, friend, or relative. If a man is needed for a short communication, a woman might stop wailing suddenly, talk in an ordinary voice, then just as quickly resume her keening. A few women at every funeral were observed who were much more totally involved and did not break up their wailing when asked to do something else. Sometimes these wails of the women become songs with words. This is less true at funerals of men where if it happens the song or chant says over and over again, "He was a good man." For a dead woman the words are also, "She was a good woman," but an added verse, especially if the dead woman was not very old, refers to the hard life of a woman and how long and unending are her chores. There is a definite implication here that the heavy burdens of womanhood can bring an early death.

This, then is the Kanuri life cycle; it is adapted to Bornu society and the historical development of that society. The fact that the household is the major unit of social organization means that people of different ages are constantly in touch with one another. Even though those in all age groups have many friends of their own age, they associate freely and easily with people of all age groups within their household where membership crosses generation lines. This means that younger age groupings are constantly learning the ways of behaving and thinking of those older than themselves and almost automatically know how to act as they grow up. By contrast in many western societies interaction between generations is extremely difficult, and each generation seems to be developing an almost semi-separate culture whose intricacies must be learned after one has joined that particular age group. Because western schooling has not yet separated an entire generation from their parents, there is little room among the Kanuri for many discontinuities in learning, and therefore in hopes, fears, and aspirations on the part of each successive generation. Obviously this has produced and helps to maintain much of the stability in Kanuri society, and as such it is a key factor when we wish to ask questions about conditions of change in the entire society of Bornu.

5

The Economic Life

NO MATTER WHERE or who they are the members of every human society must have some means by which they obtain the material goods and services deemed valuable and important to their way of life. How these goods are produced, distributed, and consumed forms the basis of the economic system of any society. However, for our present purposes the details of production are beside the point, for they deal with the local technology rather than the economy in the sense that this economy is part of the social system. Therefore, I will restrict the present chapter to the various units of Kanuri economy and its interrelationships which provide the means by which economic life is successfully carried on in Bornu.

The Kanuri do not have factories to produce goods, there are only a few large trading companies, and there are even fewer large institutional consumers of goods and services such as hospitals, schools, factories, armed forces, hotels, and so on. The bulk of the people is spread out over the entire area of Bornu in small towns and hamlets, and even in the few cities the basic economic facts of life for most of the households are very similar to those throughout the entire area. Villages and hamlets are only economic units to the extent that they have boundaries, and all the land is held by virtue of one's residence in a particular village or hamlet. However towns do not act corporately for most economic purposes. That is to say they do not buy and sell things as units, they do not organize the production of goods as units, nor do they organize the distribution of goods and services within or between villages as units. The only level at which this is done consistently throughout the society is at the level of the household whose members do form themselves into a unit of production and consumption.

It is important to remember from Chapter 3 that a household is not the same thing as the family. Very high divorce and fairly high mobility of the household members in general means that the people living in a Kanuri household can and do change a great deal over time. The economic life of the household, however, may not have changed at all. Just as personnel turnover does not change the basic nature of a business firm in western society, so does it have little effect on the jobs to be done and how they are carried out in a Kanuri household.

There are other units in the economy, and as we describe the major features of this system, these will become clear since many of them are still essentially related to the household. Within the household there are individual producers who may sometimes maintain independent or semi-independent economic activities from others in the household. Again, above the household level there are often groups of households whose members, or more often whose household heads, are linked together in common economic activities. Finally in the traditional system there is the market place and its relationship to the household and to other markets. Outside of this set of interrelated units, but articulated with them, are the modern activities provided for by the government and the large commercial enterprises that have been in Bornu now for nearly half a century.

The Household as an Economic Unit

Most Kanuri households have from three to ten people living inside the compound walls. As we have seen, each person, except small children, has his or her own sleeping hut, and the major group in the household is generally a family. In the larger cities, especially the capital of Maiduguri, larger households are more common and often household heads rent out a sleeping hut or two to strangers who live semi-independently from the rest of the household. As households change through time their members, and most importantly their male members, both kin and nonkin clients, move out and establish their own residences either close by or some distance away. Whether or not they maintain close contacts with their former compound head depends to a large extent on the economic relationships being established and maintained or broken when the independent residence is set up.

The division of labor within the household depends for the most part on the sex and age of its members. The women cook, draw water for the household, help on the farm if they are not in seclusion, raise garden crops in the compound, thresh, pound and grind grain, sweep and clean the compound, tend the young children, keep chickens and ducks, and engage in petty trade, usually of a retail nature. Some women specialize in creating the elaborate Kanuri women's coiffure. Others make pots, while still others make baskets, and a few are professional entertainers who work with male drummers and praise-singers. Generally, however, these specialized activities are not common, and most men when asked about their wives claim they have no occupation besides that of being a housewife. The major tasks then are cooking and preparing food, helping on the farm, and raising children. In all these jobs younger girls help out and are under the authority of the older women who organize this work in the compound.

Men engage in politics, farm, dye, build, work metals, tan animal hides, work leather, buy, sell and slaughter cattle and smaller livestock, tailor, embroider, make hats and musical instruments, trade, weave mats, and work as laborers. They are also religious specialists, barbers, carpenters, mechanics, clerks, civil servants, and hold a host of newly introduced jobs of European origin as well as being tax payers. It is no exaggeration to say that the economy is controlled almost totally by men. The household head dispenses all incoming cash and kind resulting from craft or farm work, although a woman may keep and do as she pleases with the proceeds of her small garden inside the compound. The household head doles out the money weekly to his wives for petty market purchases and does all major purchases of food and clothing on his own. He also pays for ceremonies, transportation, and most of the gift-giving engaged in by himself and others in the household. Except for the sale of cooked food, pottery production, and female hair dressing, men control all income producing work of any kind in the entire society.

Households as Consumers

Almost all people in Bornu use, obtain, or eat the things they need because they are members of particular households or are related to a nearby household as a subordinate of its household head. The patterns of consumption vary enormously from that of a rural peasant to that of a wealthy trader or political leader in the city. However, the vast bulk of the population stays within a fairly uniform range that involves a relatively low level of consumption. Most families, especially those in rural areas, eat two meals a day; one between 8:00 and 9:00 A.M. and the other in the early evening between 8:00 and 9:00 P.M. Men of the compound and their male friends eat together while the women eat separately. Smaller snacks are eaten during the day, and in the city it is common to eat more often especially among salaried workers who return home for breakfast about 9:00 to 9:30 A.M. and finish the work day at 2:00 to 2:30 P.M. at which time they eat a noon-day meal. The average rural household consumes about eight pounds of millet (the staple grain food) every day, or about one and a half tons per year. The millet comes from farm products used by the household plus any buying that has to be done to augment this. For those few at the higher end of the social scale food bills can be enormous. One political leader in the capital claims that during his heyday he used to feed as many as seventy people a day and had to have a very smoothly-running household to get this much food processed and ready for his guests on a daily basis. In the ordinary peasant household men give their wives money on a weekly basis to purchase condiments for the staple food and sometimes meat as well although many of the richer men prefer to buy meat themselves. The money, usually anywhere from thirty cents to about $1.50 is given to the wife, or to each wife, or sometimes to the senior wife who then divides it among the co-wives.[1]

To an outsider Kanuri food seems almost infinitely expandable. I have often watched one bowl of food brought into the presence of a household head. He would glance around at the half dozen or so of us present and then ask us to join him, as he had to do by custom. On the other hand household heads have complained to me that they feed too many. "But what can we do?" they say, friends and would-be clients or subordinates know when food is to be brought, and they simply appear, at which point custom forces the host to be gracious. Those who eat continually at a friend's or a relative's house are in his debt and he may use their services as he wishes. This is one of the principal means by which clientship starts to operate. If the client eats with the patron, and the patron asks for services, and if both are satisfied, the relationship soon becomes an established one.

Clothing, like food, is in the hands of the household head although, and as

---

[1] Nigerian money is in pounds, shillings, and pence. I have translated values here at the rate of $2.80 American to £1 Nigerian.

in the case of food, he is always pressured to obtain and distribute more than he can afford. At harvest time, or major religious ceremonies during the year, and at celebrations of *rites de passage* by household members, new clothing is in order and is expected by everyone. Clients and subordinates in nearby households expect gifts of clothing as well. Wealthy men may find it necessary to purchase several hundred men's robes a year just to satisfy their many dependents; on the other hand, a normal peasant householder can usually get by annually with under a half a dozen for male household members including himself and a similar number of women's robes for his wives.

Household heads must also organize and pay for repairs to compound walls and sleeping huts, fuel and equipment for cooking fires, and kerosene for the lamps. They must supply as well the ladies of the household with money for their fortnightly hair styling, perfumes, pomade for rubbing on their skin, and kola nuts. When someone is sick, they must consult the religious practitioner and the native doctor who diagnose the case, start the necessary prayers, and sell charms to effect a cure. Besides all this they must enter into community life, go to the weddings, naming ceremonies of friends, and have these friends come to their own ceremonies. Each time they attend affairs they and their household members must give gifts to those responsible for the ceremony. The more a man gives and the more often he goes to such ceremonies, the more successful and wealthy and contact-laden he is reputed to be. Most people are prudent and do not go beyond their means. Indeed the Kanuri term for "spendthrift" translates literally as "one who goes to many ceremonies."

Consumption at the household level is organized by the household head and carried out under his guidance and control. He is constantly purchasing more so he can distribute it more generously to more people; yet for the ordinary household the bulk of the expenditure, roughly sixty percent of the household's earning power, is for food, and the next largest item is clothing, at about fifteen percent. This leaves approximately twenty-five percent of the household earning capacity to take care of everything in cash and kind beyond the simple necessities of food and clothing.[2]

Households as Producers

Kanuri production is tied traditionally to two interrelated factors in the physical and social environment of Bornu. These are, first, the geographical and ecological characteristics of the area, and secondly, the way in which agricultural and nonagricultural pursuits complement one another in the economy. The Bornu area has a short rainy season from June to September and crop production is carried out during these months. Planting begins about the time of the first rains, and the first hoeing takes place shortly afterward. The second hoeing is carried on from the beginning of October to the end of November. Each hoeing requires between two to three weeks' work and harvesting may take as long as a month to a month and a half. Between these periods, beyond occasional scrutiny to see that straying

---

[2] These data and much of the other material for this chapter were obtained (a) from detailed budget studies in a small sample of twenty-two rural households, and (b) from a less detailed survey of seventy-five rural households in three villages in the Magumeri area.

cattle have not broken into and eaten the produce, very little work is required in cultivating crops. Thus work on crop production is concentrated into less than six months leaving the rest of the year free for other activities.

Although almost all Kanuri households obtain some food and some cash from their farm plots, the amount of farming varies from person to person, from village to village, and even for the same person from season to season. In the city, many people have dropped farming and manage to earn enough cash income to furnish their needs from the market. In the villages some households, usually in areas of good soil and water supply, produce agricultural surpluses, while in other areas the farm work provides only part of the household needs. Again some farmers tend to produce fairly similar amounts of grain crops per year while others fluctuate, so that they produce practically nothing some years and large bounties a few years later. Increased prices of ground-nuts and guinea corn stimulate greater household farming activities while trade and other nonfarming activities may interfere with a man's farming. Sickness in the compound as well as blight and soil depletion tend to decrease agricultural proceeds, and finally in the rural areas increase or decrease in household size, especially in the number of wives, all tend to affect the fluctuation of crop proceeds from one household to another or within the same household over time. People who report themselves to be primarily farmers produce more than those who report themselves to be craftsmen, although for the Magumeri area the difference, when measured, does not seem to be very great. On the other hand, traders and political and religious specialists seem to produce approximately one quarter to one third as much on their farms as other people, and many in this category do not farm at all.

The importance of wives has already been noted. The number of wives available to any cultivator, as well as the number of his male subordinates in the household, is the major factor affecting crop production. The high divorce rate makes this primary source of labor somewhat unpredictable for each farmer. On the other hand it also helps to stabilize marriage. Thus the more men depend upon help from their wives the less likely they are to divorce them, although their efforts in this direction are never completely successful and the insecurity of farm help is always there. The insecurity can be alleviated by using sons or clients or laborers, all of whom require payment in some way for their help. All rural Kanuri at times help their neighbors, their relatives, or friends to farm and often a group of such men get together to help one another in a cooperative work gang and then reciprocate by helping each other in turn. Thus although many Kanuri do move around in Bornu, farming favors the most stable who can build up social relations in one place that can be utilized in the form of labor to offset the possible insecurity caused by the ever-present high divorce rate.

To make the situation more complicated many Kanuri are not rooted in the land emotionally. It is part of both the traditional and contemporary Kanuri conception of getting ahead in the world that personal advancement is not to be found in farming. Achievement in Bornu is seen as stemming out of profitable social relationships and more recently western schooling. If it is judged to be personally profitable for an individual to leave his farm work in order to become someone's client, there is little hesitation. Men asked me to take them on as clients and give them some money for trading purposes. They offered to travel anywhere in Bornu and then bring me the profits whether or not they had crops growing and whether or not they had labor to carry on the cultivation. If I asked them what would happen to their farm they showed little concern and said merely that they farm because they can do nothing else. The implication is that if they had anything better to do they would stop farming immediately.

Land for agriculture is not scarce in Bornu and all settlements except the capital city have plenty of free or unused land within their boundaries. Adjacent to a Kanuri village or hamlet are the farm plots of long-term members of the settlement and their descendants who have inherited these "house-farms" as they are called in Kanuri because they represent land attached to households. These plots are always bounded and often fertilized by the village sheep and goats. In Magumeri house-farms extend in a circle around the village for a radius of about three quarters of a mile. Outside this circle are isolated farm plots dotted here and there and free land as well as pasture land. Ownership is obtained by clearing such land after having registered this intent with the village head, by inheriting a plot, or by having been given it by the previous owner. The Kanuri see house-farm land as symbolizing long-term and stable association with a village or city, while bush farms, although everyone has a few such plots, mean transience or newness because the household head who farms only these does not yet have any farm plots identified with his compound so that people can say, "There is Modu's house, his house-farms are in such-and-such a spot." Instead they say, "That is Modu, he has moved into so-and-so's house or built a house near so-and-so, and has cleared a few new farm plots a mile or two to the south of town."

An interesting and yet difficult question is that of land ownership. The way in which land is owned can be seen in those practices associated with acquisition and transfer. Anyone can clear new land or land that has been unclaimed for many years. He should report this to his local political leader whose permission is always granted if there are no known claims on the property. Again a man may go to the local political leader and ask where he can farm; he is then directed to available plots on the advice of the leader. Or land may be inherited, usually in the male line, or acquired as a gift from a friend, or it can even be sold. Political leaders sometimes try to exert themselves in being party to all land transfers so that their permission becomes part of the transaction, and they feel they have a legitimate right to do so when the previous owner has used the land for a short period. The difficulty here is that there is no definite rule to tell the Kanuri how long a man should use a piece of land during his own lifetime before he has a total right to transfer it to anyone else. On the other hand, they believe that once land has been inherited it is the property of the family, and decisions about its use and transfer are primarily in the hands of the owners. In practice the Kanuri always hold land because they are using it, having cleared it, inherited it, or come to some agreement over it with the previous owner. In the latter case this could mean anything from an outright sale, practiced more near the larger cities, to an agreement over it with the user who gives the previous owner some percentage of the crop. The system works well when household heads as land owners and users have good working relations with their local political leaders. If this is not the case, then political leaders often insist on helping to make decisions about the land and its ultimate transfer whether it has been held for a short time or a much longer one. I have seen or been told of many political leaders who rubber stamp decisions about land transfer, simply registering the fact and witnessing its legality. In some cases, however, there is interference, and it is generally discovered when this happens that there have been some previous difficulties in the owner's relationship to the political leader.

Farm plots are generally used for periods of four to eight years. Then they are allowed to lie fallow for about the same length of time. Everyone in the community knows a fallow field and its owner, and there would be trouble if someone tried to use one of these without the owner's permission. If fallow land is unused because the owner has moved away or has given up farming, then the land reverts to the common disposal of the community as a whole. The political leader can then allot these lands to newcomers or other community members, although he would generally be careful to check claims on them by previous owners and their relatives before doing this.

In summary, from the point of view of the people themselves, there are four different kinds of land around a Kanuri village. First, there is land owned outright by the household head over which he has complete authority. Secondly, there is land that has been cleared by a household head or that he was given the right to use by his local leader and which may become totally his or that of his heirs after long years of use and/or inheritance. Thirdly there is resting land, which is a farm plot that has been in use but whose depleted soil the owner will likely use again. If he moves away without trying to dispense with any of these plots then they revert to free land. Finally, there is free unused land around the settlement that can be used for newcomers or those trying to expand their holdings. As far as ownership is concerned, about sixty percent of all land in Magumeri was obtained through inheritance. The remaining forty percent was almost all new land cleared outside the present circumference òf farm plots in which the plots had been registered with the village head whose permission had been granted. The important thing to remember about this system is that it works. Litigation over land in Magumeri had to do mostly with what we call "trespassing." People were brought to the courts because they (usually their livestock) had infringed on someone's right to land. There was very little difficulty in general over transfers. People knew what rights were held and how they could transfer these rights to others.

Except for the few farmers who produce either specialized crops like yams or tobacco and then market them, most Kanuri have a dry season occupation such as craftwork, trade, or a service occupation such as native doctoring or barbering. These they view as an occupation, while farming, unless it is the only specialty carried out, is viewed as an important side line. As we have seen in the chapter on the life cycle, recruitment into an occupation is carried on by an apprenticeship system within the household organization. This is even the case for some western types of occupation such as truck driving, and it only recedes in importance when western type schooling is involved.

Traditionally, occupations in Bornu have been organized under head men in each settlement and under an overall head man for the entire occupation who lived in the capital city. Today the traditional occupations such as blacksmith, leather worker, butcher, and so on still have such an organization, although the privileges and duties of a head man are very few and do not extend beyond his local settlement. Nevertheless, men in Magumeri who are butchers, blacksmiths or dyers, and so on, report that if they visit the capital of Maiduguri they often go to pay their respects to the Maiduguri head of their own occupation. People felt that rural heads of occupations should always do this, and everyone else should try to do it now and then. Local heads of occupations, no matter where they live, usually do have some privileges. Thus in larger villages and cities, the head butcher has one day a week, not market day, on which his meat alone is sold in villages. In Magumeri the head butcher receives a small commission on all hides and skins sold by the village's butchers.

Very often those in similar occupations live close to one another within a village, and some small hamlets are made up of people devoted almost exclusively to one craft activity. This reflects the fact that sons tend to settle in the vicinity of their fathers especially when they take up the same occupation. Since this is also true of many clients and apprentices, who are non-kin, it is often quite normal to see a hamlet or a ward of a larger village composed of people most of whom practice the same dry season activity.

In analytical terms almost all of Kanuri craft production is characterized by simple technology, cottage industry organization in the same household or a group of closely related households, and by its interrelations with regional and even international competition. Let us go over these points one by one.

Only the simplest tools are required to produce everything made in Bornu, and the materials for these can often be obtained locally. Methods of production are slow and laborious. For example, an ordinary blacksmith working at home, as they all do, can make from three to five hoes a day; or a dyer working over his dye vat can color five or six robes in a busy day with no disturbances. A potter makes from ten to twenty pots a week, depending upon the type of pots being turned out. Compared to the productivity of more industrialized workers in Africa itself or other parts of the world, such outputs are almost infinitesimal. Production itself is almost always carried on in small groups located inside the household of a craftworker. In this sense Bornu craft production is of the cottage industry type. Sometimes a group of craftsmen work together in their own ward of the town, especially when the group includes a number of agnatically related kinsmen among its members. This means that a craftsman spends his working hours at home or close by in a neighbor's household, and these neighbors are often close kin. In some special cases craft work is organized along some other lines. Thus the blind people, who often live together in a ward of their own, produce rope and then sell it in one section of the market. It is an occupation that can be practiced by the blind and affords them some means of livelihood in the community.

Unlike food production in which the Bornu area provides almost everything they require in the way of staples, Kanuri crafts have never been totally self-sufficient. Thus iron for blacksmiths, dyes for clothes, paper, textiles, or glass beads have always come from outside Bornu. Furthermore there has always been competition between locally manufactured articles and those from other parts of the Sudan. This works both ways so that Bornu knives are accepted and coveted items in many markets all over the Sudan, while leather work from Kano can be seen all over Bornu and is always in high demand. On a more local level in a small village like Magumeri, craftwork from other villages almost always finds its way into the local market to compete with items produced in Magumeri. Such openness means that craftsmen must sustain any and all competition from the import of goods into Nigeria. Thus native weaving has almost disappeared, as it has been unable to withstand the onslaught of milled cotton cloth from Europe and Japan.

Given the household nature and low productivity of most craft production in Bornu, it is interesting to ask whether many households can sustain themselves by relying on the proceeds. In rural Magumeri and surrounding villages craftsmen estimated their earnings per week from craftwork in both the dry and the wet seasons. When we compared these figures to the expenses of these same households in terms of food, clothing, ceremonies, taxes and so forth, we found that craftwork most often provides for about forty to fifty percent of the household expenses on an annual basis. In other words for rural producers craftwork is an important source of income but does not provide for the household's entire economic needs. This is why almost all Kanuri outside the capital city are farmers *and* blacksmiths, or farmers *and* calabash makers, or farmers *and* dyers, etc. On the other hand three kinds of people in rural Magumeri and its surrounding villages invariably get most of their income from non-farming activities. These are the political specialists or those connected by salary to the native administration, to a lesser extent the religious specialists, and to a still lesser extent many of the traders. These men tend to get higher cash incomes than the ordinary peasant craftsmen and thus do less farming.

When Kanuri craftsmen estimate why their productivity in household crafts goes up or down, they give a number of reasons, but the one that comes up over and over again concerns the loss or gain of helpers who either live in the household or close by. In other words the number of wives, followers, clients, sons, and so on that a craftsman can depend upon to help him is in their view the largest determinant of productivity for craft enterprise.

By way of illustration let us look at a couple of cases so that we can see some of these generalizations as they apply to the lives of the people themselves.

KA'ANAMI, THE CALABASH MAKER   Ka'anami lives in a compound with four other people: his wife and infant daughter, his younger brother (same father, same mother), and his father's older sister. The compound, although fully enclosed with grass mat walls, is next door to and opens into the compound of Ka'anami's father. Dolo, the younger brother, has his own farm plot on which he grows ground-nuts for cash, and he makes a few calabashes now and then. The old woman, Palmatta, makes pots and cooks her own food. Dolo eats with his older brother, his father, or is given cooked food by the old woman. He used to help his father a great deal more than he does now but he still contributes now and then to both his father's and his brother's farm labor. He is doing much less of this at present and is instead contemplating marriage. He is discussing this with his brother who relays the information to their father. This involves the possibility of setting up his own household close by. Dolo still runs messages for his father and like Ka'anami feels that his father is head of a group of contiguous households within their ward of the village. Ka'anami has a "far-farm" or bush farm about three quarters of a mile south of Magumeri and three "house-farm" plots close to the hamlet of Fulongo, about two miles south of Magumeri, where he and his father used to live before the entire family moved to Magumeri. He generally harvests from twelve to fourteen bags of millet which he stores, and four to five bags of ground-nuts which he sells for cash.

To make calabashes Ka'anami buys dried half-gourds, then scrapes the excess vegetable matter from the inside and burns designs on the outer surface with hot irons. The tools are simple, merely a number of wood-handled iron blades made by the local blacksmith. Add to this charcoal for the fire to heat the irons, and the list of materials necessary for his occupation is complete. In the dry season when he is not planting Ka'anami makes about two calabashes a day on Fridays and Saturdays—the two days before Magumeri's market day, on Sunday. On Monday, Tuesday, and Wednesday he goes to other markets or makes calabashes on commission for people who want special orders. On the average he makes about fifteen calabashes per month for the four months of the wet season. For the dry season he estimates that his productivity goes up to about twenty a month. This means that on his own Ka'anami produces about 250 to 300 calabashes a year. If this sounds like a lot, it must be remembered that he sells them for anything between forty cents and seventy-five cents each. Subtract from this the cost of the gourds (about fifteen cents each) and add the fact that some weeks he doesn't sell all his wares, and it is easy to realize that the entire proceeds of Ka'anami's craft-work do not produce much beyond $150 to $200 per year in income.

Ka'anami's father, his father's younger brother, and one of his father's younger brother's sons, plus a man who for years has been a subordinate to Ka'anami's father all live in adjoining compounds and all make calabashes. Each compound is to a large extent independent, yet all originally were under the guidance and direction of Ka'anami's father who considers himself the leader of this group of households. If higher political authorities in the village wish to contact anyone in this group they invariably do so through Ka'anami's father thus recognizing his leadership and giving it legitimacy in the community.

In summary this way of productive life is far removed from the regular eight-hour day of the industrial worker. Ka'anami could no doubt produce more calabashes if he worked more rapidly and for longer hours and more days a week. But he doesn't have to—his efforts support his family and himself, and Ka'anami likes his life. He enjoys sitting in an entrance hut in his part of town with friends and relatives, people he has known all his life, talking, joking, gossiping, and moralizing about rural events. Indeed even a casual brush with Ka'anami's life indicates that he sits talking and resting in the shade for long periods of time. But he works too, and when he does he often sits around a common fire at his father's entrance hut with the other calabash makers talking or singing softly while each man looks to his own hot irons and unfinished gourds. Even when he works alone in his own compound or with his brother Dolo, friends come to visit him, or he dandles his infant daughter on his lap while cleaning out a gourd. His family, his friends and neighbors, and his fellow workers, are all interwoven into the pattern of his household life and his relation to the surrounding households. Thus the social and economic side of Ka'anami's life is part of the same fabric—this is the human side of cottage industry.

In the case below we see another household in which *tada njima* or client apprentices are more prominent and yet many of the same kinds of social and economic relations prevail.

MALA BUKAR, THE BUTCHER   The butcher's craft, although lucrative in relation to other activities like Ka'anami's or blacksmithing, is a low status occupation, and many butchers including Mala Bukar are quick to say that their families were not butchers in times past but conditions have forced them to "take up the knife." The craft requires anatomical knowledge of animals and a skilled use of the knife to cut and clean them. Besides this it necessitates continuous relations with cattle owners, many of whom are Shuwa and Fulani nomads who wander through the area.

Mala Bukar lives with his two wives, the younger of whom has a small child aged three, and two *tada njima* who are his apprentices. There are five huts in the compound, one each for the wives, one for Mala Bukar, one for the two apprentices, and one for meat storage. The apprentices are both unrelated to Mala Bukar by kinship, but both are the sons of butchers who are well known to him. The young boys explained that they wished to travel about the country before they settled down as butchers in their home villages. They treated Mala Bukar as they would their own father giving him all the subordination and respect due to a compound head. Mala Bukar's immediate neighbors, one to the north of him and one just to the east of him, are his younger brothers. One sells hides and skins, the other is a butcher and works closely with him although they generally butcher separately. They do, however, buy from nomads together, and often the younger brother looks after Mala Bukar's stall in the various markets they journey to together. The three brothers inherited their "house-farms" from their father. Mala Bukar— as the older brother who took over his father's household—took half while the other half was divided between the two younger brothers. Since then he has cleared one plot in free land far from town, and his apprentices are busy clearing a new one which Mala Bukar says is being cleared to replace an old one used for the last time several years ago (it is now fallow). The apprentices are also clearing small plots of their own near to the one they are preparing for the butcher and hope to get some extra cash from ground-nuts. Generally Mala Bukar estimates he obtained about ten bags (one ton) of millet and three bags (600 pounds) of ground-nuts.

The farm work itself is done by Mala Bukar's two wives and his apprentices who do not work together because it would be considered shameful for them to have to interact socially for any length of time. Mala Bukar decides on what is to be planted, when, and in what plots. He also decides on hoeing dates, and the time and scheduling of the harvest. The wives do less actual work in the field than many of their rural counterparts because of the apprentices, although they still take or send out cooked food to the boys during the hoeing season. Mala Bukar also gives his wives the hooves of slaughtered animals which they are able to sell for extra spending money.

The work schedule of the household is tied to the supply of Mala Bukar's meat and local demands for it. During the dry season he slaughters mostly sheep and goats while the rainy season which brings the cattle nomads is more heavily the time for beef preparation. He almost always butchers on Saturdays, the day before the village market day, and may do some more on Sunday if selling is brisk at the market. During Sunday he hears about conditions in the villages close by that have markets on Monday and Tuesday. If demand there seems promising, or if he has unsold stock, he attends the Monday and Tuesday markets as well.

Even with the apprentices, however, his turnover is not excessive. In the dry season he kills about four goats and/or sheep per week, and once in a while, usually about once a month, a beef-cow or bull. During the wet season he kills about one or two beef cattle a week. He sells the meat by strips and a very rough estimate of his income from the meat and the sale of the skin comes to approximately $450 per year. Most of the townspeople of Magumeri think of Mala Bukar as one of the wealthiest of the village's permanent residents, leaving aside the salaried officials sent out from the city who have been posted to Magumeri. However, both as we observed it, and as Mala Bukar claimed repeatedly, people begged meat from him continually for which he never received any money. In four weeks of almost continous observation I estimated he lost about ten percent of his meat this way, although he claimed it was often much higher, ranging up to forty percent on occasion. Everyone agrees that that is the price of wealth, for the Kanuri believe that the proper use of wealth is its distribution to one's dependents and to the community at large in order that one may achieve fully the acclaim and prestige that wealth confers. If Mala Bukar hoarded his earnings to buy more animals and obtain more apprentices and thus increase his productivity, people would see him as a foolish man who was using his wealth unproductively. Kanuri wealth should be used to enhance and maintain status, and status is achieved through supporting and creating subordinates by giving away wealth.

Distribution

Kanuri households do not produce everything they consume and thus of necessity must obtain what they need from other sources in the community. Wives are given market money weekly by their husbands to purchase ingredients for gruel as well as for their own needs. The household head, on his part, must purchase grain when his own supplies are short as well as clothing and supplies such as tools or firewood for the entire compound. Things made, produced, or purchased for trade by the household members must be sold or exchanged in order to obtain necessities not produced within the compound. This is the basic quality in Bornu out of which stems an elaborate and complicated system of trade that provides for the distribution of goods and services to those who need them, when they need them, in quantities they can afford.

Almost all households in rural Bornu, and many in the city as well, have two main marketing tasks. First the cash crop, most often ground-nuts, must be sold, and secondly the specialized production or services provided by the household must be made available to the community. Let us go over each of these briefly and then move into the market cycle itself to see how the system operates as a whole.

During the harvest season from November to January men from the city appear at every major market village in Bornu. They bring scales with them and set up temporary huts close to the nearest motor road. When a household head harvests the crop, he takes it to these "scale men" and sells it by the bag. Government inspectors are on hand to check the scales daily and the quality of the nuts as well. The scale men generally bring cloth and other import items with them so that when a householder gets his cash he can spend some of it immediately thus giving the buyer a little extra profit. For the householder this may be the largest single payment in cash he receives all year and he has made elaborate plans for its disposal. He often watches the scale men for several weeks asking questions about them from other farmers, perhaps even going to visit a few to see if he can obtain a slightly better price than that set by the government. On their side the scale men may try to buy a "future" if they see the farmer is in trouble. This involves a cash advance and a much lower final sale price which is intended to cover the greater risk by the buyer since the crop may fail. This practice is illegal, and there have been very serious attempts to stamp it out.

Craft production and special services such as religious prayers or barbering are made available in several ways. If someone needs a new hoe, or a mat, or a calabash, or the services of a religious person, he may go to that person's household and ask for it. Even in large villages whose markets are open every day it is still common to go to the household of a producer and purchase things when they are required. On the other hand for many things it is still common to go to the market and see what is available.

Markets are held weekly and referred to by the day of the week they are held in any particular village. More often than not people use this weekday as another name for the village itself. Thus in Magumeri a man says, "I am going to Thursday this Monday," meaning that on Monday he is going to Ngubbura, the village that has its market on Thursdays. Even large villages whose market places are open every day are known to have one day a week that is their "real" market day. Thus the market in Maiduguri, the capital city, is much busier on Mondays, its named market day, than during the rest of the week. The reason for this is the link-up of market villages into interlocking cycles.

The best way to understand a market cycle is to ask a Kanuri, "What markets do you visit?" He then generally gives you a village for every day in the week except for Friday, the Moslem sabbath. These are a series of villages of medium size, usually within a radius of five to ten miles from the village in which you asked the question. Not everyone goes to a market every day, but they know of one in their vicinity and may go to as many as three or four a week if they are busy trading goods. Sometimes they may visit two villages on the same market day one in one direction this week, then another one in the other direction next week, but to a remarkable degree Bornu markets do have a weekly cycle in which people can visit a market close by on any day of the six working days of the week. The reason these weekly market cycles are interlocking stems from the fact that no two villages have exactly the same cycle. Thus a man in Magumeri might go to Ardoram eight miles north of Magumeri for his Monday market, but the Magumeri man goes to Ngubbura five miles to the south of his own village for the Thursday market. On the other hand on that same day the Ardoram man goes further north to a village in *his* cycle rarely ever visited by the Magumeri people, and he in his turn does not often attend the Ngubbura market which is thirteen miles south of Ardoram. So each village has some, but not all, markets in common with others close by, and the entire countryside is linked into interlocking sets of these weekly market cycles. It is important to remember here that many people walk to market, and it is more difficult for the Ardoram man to walk the twenty-six miles to and from Ngubbura market than it is to walk the much shorter distance to his own Thursday market.

Besides the interlocking cycles of local markets many villages and all cycles have links with the larger centers of the export-import trade of Bornu Province. If there are roads, trucks bring out goods and people from the city at least once a week and take back locally produced things to the city. Where there are no roads the camel caravan and donkey load do the same job they have done for centuries. Where the market is too small or too remote, then the interlocking nature of the cycle brings and takes goods to a larger place on a main route.

Markets, especially those on motor roads, tend to set the pattern or rhythm of intersettlement communication and travel. Thus if Bukar of Magumeri wishes to take several bags of millet to Yerwa (the usual name for Maiduguri), he knows that he can get a lorry at the Thursday, Sunday, or Monday markets which will take him and his goods to the capital. Again if Bukar's sister is coming to visit him from the capital or some other distant place in Bornu, she will arrive on a market day. If a man's wife wishes to divorce him or he her, she must wait until market day to leave him in order to obtain proper transportation back to her relatives if they live in some distant part of the province. Thus the market cycle plus the presence of lorries and roads determines a large part of the rhythm of rural life and this in turn adds zest, interest, and excitement to market days. Beyond this rhythmical quality markets are also major sources of news and gossip about politics, marriages, births, circumcisions, and deaths. Pagans brew beer for sale on the local market day, and gamblers hold card games in the nearby bush area. Gambling, strangers, new bits of gossip, perhaps a new woman or two, drummers and entertainers, all contribute and create not just an ordinary day for buying and selling goods, but a festive occasion that is regarded as a welcome break or relief in the daily monotony of rural life.

Most markets have very little formal organization. Each one has its head man or "big man of the market" to whom disputes are referred, and if he cannot settle the disagreement, then it is taken to the head of the village or to the judge if the village boasts a regular Moslem court. In the capital city the market is so large and disputes so frequent that there is a special court nearby to handle market affairs. In the market itself, each variety of thing being sold has its own section, and, as in the village, the butcher's section is generally on the lee side (southwest) of the market site. In the larger villages market fees are taken from sellers who use the stalls, but this is uncommon in small centers where they just take the first one available as long as they restrict themselves to that section of the market given over to their particular type of selling.

Prices vary with the season, the time of day, and how common the item is. Taking the last point first, a fancy imported man's robe may have a relatively wide price range since not many people buy these, and the seller tries to charge as much as he can. At the other end are items like boxes of sugar cubes which everyone buys regularly. The prices of such items are well known and people do not haggle over them at all but simply give the money to the seller since both know the standard price. Some food commodities such as millet and guinea corn are sold in the Magumeri market at a flat price for a small gourd-full of grain, but the prices vary for a bag of grain over the year. In order to keep prices constant sellers simply vary the size of the gourd. In general, food prices rise during the growing season when they are scarce and fall again after harvest time, while many material items like jewelry, clothes, etc., are just the opposite, going down in price when cash is scarce and rising later when people have more money after the harvest.

The Organization of Trade

Looking at Bornu as a whole it is also important to see how trade is organized so that goods can move from one point to another as well as into and out of the society as a whole. The best terms to start with here are "retail" and "wholesale," since the Kanuri themselves see a distinction between selling to ultimate consumers as compared with selling to people who are in turn going to sell the item again. At the local level in a town like Magumeri trade is handled by retailers who sell uncooked foods, medicines, charms, medical services, building services, sundries, etc., directly to consumers and the local householders. Generally speaking goods produced locally are retailed locally, usually by the producers themselves. Thus Ka'anami sells his own calabashes, Mala Bukar his own meat, the blacksmith his own tools, and so on. However goods not produced locally such as salt, textiles, kola nuts, and European manufactured goods, are sold by wholesalers first to local retailers, then by these retailers to the local users. The wholesale relationships between buyers and sellers is a very important one and must be viewed close-up to be appreciated. Let us therefore look at it from the point of view first of the retailer, then a wholesaler, then a "financier" who uses his capital to support wholesale trade.

MOMADU, THE SALT SELLER   Momadu is about sixty years old and has lived in Magumeri for eight years. He comes originally from Hadejia to the west of Bornu where he began selling salt for an Arab trader when he was a teenager. The Arab gave him several bags of salt (100 pounds per bag) on trust, and he would sell it on the market in one-penny lots at a profit of a few shillings a bag for himself. After the salt was sold, he would pay back the Arab. Later he came to Bornu and was given credit by some of his father's brother's sons. However after a while they quarreled over the division of the profits from the salt selling, and he left this group and came to Magumeri. In Magumeri he asked the district head's wife to help him since she was known for her interest in trade. She arranged for one of her servants to go to the capital weekly and buy salt from the Levantine traders. She then distributed these to a number of people, including Momadu, who paid her when the salt was sold.

Later, when this woman moved away with her husband to another district, Momadu obtained a connection with a wealthy trader in Maiduguri with the help of the district head's wife. This trader sends out a follower each week with five bags of salt and Momadu sells this by visiting local markets during the week. His relationship to his supplier is somewhat impersonal although they trust one another and Momadu pays his respects to his supplier when visiting the city. Momadu says he does not need a very close relationship to his supplier because he already is the *tada njima* or client-follower of Kachella Abba, the head dyer of Magumeri. Momadu has no wife so he eats at Kachella Abba's house, borrows money from him without interest, runs messages for him, and helps Kachella Abba on the latter's farm. If Kachella Abba were to leave Magumeri, Monadu feels he would move with him. This would not impair his relationship to the salt supplier since that man lives in Maiduguri where he would still have to go to obtain wholesale salt. He says Kachella Abba is his "father" and he would and must serve him and give him respect even though the two men are nearly the same age.

BUKAR, THE "TADA NJIMA"   Another example of retailing that shows how it is often imbedded into a more general relationship is that of Bukar. Bukar can be seen three or four days a week walking about the village of Magumeri with a tin of cellophane-wrapped candies. One of the village's household heads goes in and out of the city regularly on messages for the native administration. When in the city he buys a tin or two of candy and brings these back to Magumeri. The boy, Bukar, is about twenty years old; he is not related by descent or marriage to the senior man but lives in his compound and is fed and clothed by the household head. When the senior rides horseback in ceremonies the boy carries his spear and walks behind the horse; he gathers grass for the horse, runs messages for the household head, carries water for the household, and works on the household farm-plots. Receipts from the candy sale are given to the household head who then gives Bukar a small amount for himself. Here the retailing of candy is only one aspect of the relationship between Bukar and his household head. He refers to his superior, the household head, as *abba njima* or father of the house, and says of him, "He is just like my father."

AJIMI, THE KOLA NUT SELLER   Next we see a wholesaler who sells directly to retailers in an ancient trade that has always allowed for middlemen by the score because of the vast distances over which it is carried out. Ajimi is a young man of twenty-five or twenty-six who lives with his brothers in a small hamlet just outside Magumeri. For the six to nine months a year when farming is slack, and intermittently while he is farming, Ajimi sells kola nuts to local retailers. Ajimi gets the money from his father's older brother in the city and then buys a *kwando,* a large rope wrapped package of nuts. A kwando costs about sixty to seventy dollars and contains roughly 7000 to 8000 nuts. He buys the nuts from traders in the city who ship them into Maiduguri from other parts of Nigeria and West Africa.

Ajimi visits three or four of these traders regularly about twice a month in the dry season. He always goes to all of them, inspects their goods, talks prices, and then decides where to place his order. He does this for two reasons. First there is always some variety in price and quality and he must try to get the best he can of both. Secondly, by going to these same suppliers, among dozens of possible ones, he feels he can build up their confidence in him by selling his stuff well and steadily. Indeed, several of the suppliers have on occasion given him an extra kwando on credit and he kept the profits for himself.

Generally Ajimi brings the nuts back in time for Magumeri Sunday market and attends the Thursday and Monday markets as well at nearby towns. He can sell a kwando to retailers in about two weeks and make a profit of about thirty dollars, half of which he gives to his father's older brother who supplied the original money. Thus he makes about fifteen dollars for two weeks of wholesaling—if he is lucky and sagacious in his relations to retailers. Retailers can go to several suppliers like Ajimi. They decide on the basis of quality of the nuts, on the price, and whether they can obtain credit when they need it. The most flexible and negotiable of these is credit, and Ajimi has his most difficult time trying to compete on this level and still make a profit. He will not give credit to strangers, but must have done business with the man successfully or have some previous knowledge of him, his family, his agnates, or any one else who would be responsible for him if he were taken into court for a bad debt. Nevertheless, with each retailer taking about two to four dollars worth of nuts it takes only a few bad debts to whittle away his fifteen dollar profit into a loss, and he has had a number of these on which it took several later trips to recoup his losses. Ajimi, however, is very philosophical and entertains his friends for hours telling stories about his bad debts to point up the moral that a kola nut seller's life is not a happy one.

AJIMI'S UNCLE   Finally let us look at Ajimi's uncle, his father's older brother who lives in the city and runs, because of his access to liquid capital, a relatively large trading organization along traditional lines.

Ajimi's uncle is a man of fifty-five years who has three wives and a concubine as well as a son and a younger brother's son living in his large compound in Maiduguri. He generally has several *tada njima* living in the compound, and in the near vicinity are those of his other married *tada njima* who are part of his organization.

His mode of operation is fairly simple; he gives out money to men like Ajimi to trade with, and then takes one half or more of the profits. Some of these men are connected by kinship to the uncle; others, indeed most of them, are not. Those who are not, start out in his compound as low status *tada njima;* they carry water, cut grass for the horses, run messages, and so on. For this they receive their food, shelter, clothing, and a little pocket money. If over a period of one to two years they prove respectable and trustworthy, Ajimi's uncle gives them some money and sends them out to trade, usually with someone more experienced at first, then on their own. The following list indicates both the range and number of his enterprises:

1. Two men buy millet in Geidam for sale in Maiduguri going to the Geidam market once every week or two.

2. One man sells cloth in Damasac. The cloth is supplied to him by Ajimi's uncle who buys it in larger quantities for sale in several places. This same man is given money to buy onions and ship them to Damasac where they are scarce and high priced.

3. One man buys fish at Abadan on Lake Chad and sells it in Maiduguri.

4. Another man buys natron in Bama (to the southeast of Bornu) for sale in Maiduguri.

5. Several (from one to three) buy cattle in Bornu and sell them in Kano.

6. Several (one to three) buy cattle in Bornu and sell them in Makurdi.

7. One man purchases butter in Damaturu (Fulani country) and sells it in Maiduguri.

8. One (Ajimi) sells kola nuts in Magumeri and used to buy ground-nuts for sale in the capital.

The organization involves anywhere from eleven to sixteen men (the number varies over time) and their families, and probably involves a turnover of about $1200 to $1500 per month with a maximum profit margin of anywhere from thirty to forty percent on the investment. By Bornu standards Ajimi's uncle is a wealthy man and can well afford his car, chauffeur, and new cement-block compound with electricity and running water. Besides the scale of his operation which is quite large relative to Bornu enterprise in general, his way of organizing things is also typically Kanuri. Instead of an office building with secretaries, dictaphones, telephones, the uncle has built up a series of relationships among a set of dependents. These relationships are modelled on and grew out of exactly the same kinds of relations that exist in the Kanuri father-son relationship within a Kanuri household.

The remainder of Bornu trade is handled through a system of small and large companies. The large companies are European in origin, and until a few years ago each handled as much of the trade as possible. Today these large enterprises are increasingly African staffed, usually with southern Nigerians, and each tends to specialize in a few particular lines of the export-import trade. Besides these large enterprises there are small "canteens" (stores) run by Levantine traders and now increasingly by Kanuri traders themselves. These shops obtain stocks from the larger companies and sell to both consumers and wholesalers who hope to sell in smaller quantities.

In recent years the pattern of local economic life has changed but little. However, in the Bornu economy as a whole several new lines of development have started that are a far cry from the past. To the north of the capital city of Maiduguri in an area marked "industrial" on the provincial engineer's maps there is now a modern ground-nut oil mill and further to the east of this a large modern abattoir. In future years food processing and even manufacturing plants will appear in this area of the city. Secondly, the capital city itself is experiencing a building boom as the wealthy replace old mud houses with new ones made of concrete block. This plus the continual expansion of government buildings has produced a lucrative building trade. The local Bornu emirate government has in the past few years decided to spread its contracts out among many aspiring young building contractors, thus producing not one or two large companies but a growing number of small entrepreneurs who are gaining experience in business. This has also led to a local expansion of the concrete block industry which can easily be set up along the river where the sand is available and hand labor can be used in conjunction with cheap steel molds for making the concrete block.

Finally wealthy Kanuri men in the political system and in trade are beginning to look at the possibilities of investment as a form of wealth production. Some are buying property in the city for the rent income, or building on the land and then renting it; others or sometimes the same men are buying up adjoining small farms to the southeast of the city and turning them into mango and lemon orchards. One of these has even invested in a concrete block house at the back of his orchard that he intends to turn into a modern chicken farm with imported hens and roosters from the United States.

All of these developments seem to point away from household economy toward wages, urbanization, and the impersonality of western society in its workaday life. Will it happen? When will it happen? These are questions upon whose answer rests an entire way of life, for today the Bornu economy is essentially as described in this chapter yet these roots of change are growing points that are encouraged by the national and local leaders and by the western educational system. How much they will in fact transform the local life is a matter for future research.

6

The Political Organization

THE POLITICAL LIFE of Bornu ties togther the entire society into one overall unit so that it has an identity. As far as we know this has been the case for centuries and still is today, so that, although the Kanuri people see themselves and their society as many things, they view it primarily or basically as a political entity. To the people who live there Bornu represents a culture, a language, an ancient history, but more than anything else it represents a kingdom, or sovereign realm whose definition is political. Thus whether anyone belongs to it or not, and how one should behave within its boundaries depends first and foremost on its organization as a polity, that is, as a system in which there are recognized and legitimate means of distributing authority and making decisions at all levels of the society.

Authority distinctions are present in all organizations, and from this point of view all organizations have a political aspect. However, for our purposes it is easier to limit the discussion to the means by which decisions are made and carried out in those particular sectors of social life having some territorial or bureaucratic identity as sub-parts of the emirate government of Bornu. This excludes such things as trade groupings, like that of Ajimi's uncle described in the last chapter in which there is some hierarchy of authority, but which may not be, and often is not, located in one place. It also means that what we are discussing is a system, since each of its parts is clearly connected to the other to form a working whole. Like most other aspects of Bornu life, this system starts with the household as a basic particle and then builds onto it. It is a complicated and interwoven structure of an ancient, majestic, and yet contemporary kingdom whose stability and adaptability are monuments to men's striving for these illusive goals.

Households, Wards, and Hamlets

As we have seen in Chapter 3 a household can expand and become a group of linked households under the superior authority of a senior man. When a young man, or a man's younger brother, or his apprentice or client, wishes to get married he must decide where he will set up a house. There are three possible alternatives: (a) he can bring his wife into the house of his father or older brother, or patron whoever the superior man might be; (b) he can set up his own compound close by; or (c) he can move further away and become independent or subordinate to someone else. The decision depends upon whether or not the young man is benefiting from the previous relationship, in which case he usually stays in or near the original compound, or whether he believes himself to be suffering from it, in which case he moves or tries to move away, or near to someone more powerful, influential, and economically beneficent with whom he can associate. The decision is often a very complicated one because myriads of other factors enter into it. Thus if there is a large age discrepancy between a younger man and his older brother, and the father is dead, the younger one may feel that his older brother will never treat him as a man but always as a "young boy." Or if there are brothers and some are full (same mother, same father) while some are half (only one parent in common) then the half brothers are less close and are usually linked to different groups of people through their mothers. One young man told me confidentially that he was worried about whether his father would continue to be successful and whether he should not try to use some of his father's powerful connections in Bornu to become the client of a more important person whose position was even more impressive and more secure than that of his own parents. On the other hand many people would speak about leaving home and setting up households on their own or under influential men and never seem to get around to doing it. When asked about this they replied that this was their home, these were their relatives, and whether it was beneficial or not they ought to stay with their kinsfolk. For them blood is thicker than water, that is to say, they feel their roots in a kinship unit must be the eventual determinant of where they spend their lives.

It is these processes of household growth, and associations between households, that underlie the formation of small-scale political units in Kanuri society. The process can best be seen by observing a real life situation. About three miles southwest of Magumeri is the small hamlet of Gworongo (population circa 250–300) which falls within the boundaries of Magumeri village area. Surrounding the hamlet are small bramble-fenced plots of a special crop called *gworongo* which gives the hamlet its name. This plant is used by women as a stimulant and cosmetic along with tobacco flowers. In 1953 one of these farmers, a man named Aji, moved out of the hamlet and set up a compound near his plots of gworongo. He says he wished to be closer to his fields; others gossiped that he had quarreled with the hamlet head of Gworongo over taxes. With him moved his two wives, a younger brother, and the latter's wife, and two unmarried sons. One of these sons left about a year later to go and live in Maiduguri with his father's younger brother. The other son married in 1957 and brought his wife to live in the compound near his father. A stranger to Gworongo hamlet arrived in 1954 and cut a bush farm for himself about one mile to the north of the settlement. He had no wife at the time and asked Aji if he could build a hut near the new settlement and take his meals in Aji's compound. For this hospitality he helped Aji on the *gworongo* plots, prepared household fences, and sometimes gathered grass for Aji's horse. He has since married with both a loan and some gifts from Aji and is now a settled member of the new "community-in-the-becoming." He says that Aji is his *abba njima*, and he is a *tada njima* or client of the settlement head. All residents of this new settlement look upon its founder as their local leader. Disputes between members are always taken to Aji before going to any higher authorities while disputes with outsiders follow the general Bornu rule of going first to a political leader superior in rank to both participants. The new settlement does not have a name; however in all likelihood if it continues to grow and Aji's place is taken by one of his heirs, either his brother or his son, it will be called Aji or Ajiri after its founder. At present Aji collects taxes from the men of the new community, and these are taken by the hamlet head of Gworongo to the head of Magumeri village area. Aji hopes that one day he will be able to take the taxes directly to Magumeri, thus helping to indicate his equal political status to that of the hamlet head of Gworongo. When that happens he will be a recognized bullama or head man of a hamlet or ward. He tries to take disputes directly to Magumeri village, but in 1957 this was not accepted and the hamlet head of Gworongo was invariably called to sit in on such discussions.

The same process can be seen operating in larger villages. In Magumeri village itself one ward under its bullama (ward or hamlet head) was, in 1957, becoming large enough so that people were beginning to speak of the possibility of its splitting into two under the old bullama and a new one. In the ward a man named Kachella has under his authority the compounds of several younger full brothers, three of his sons two of whom are married, several nephews, and a few unrelated clients who say they are his *tada njima*. He collects taxes from these compounds and takes the money directly to the village head of Magumeri. However he recognizes the authority of the present ward head in settling disputes and always consults the latter first before taking the matter to a higher authority. One of his sons has married a girl from the household of the ward head and this helps link the two households. The ward head seems tolerant of the rising power and influence of his neighbor and always consults him on any major decision affecting the ward. Eventually however, if the set of linked households under the authority of Kachella continues to expand, then he will become a recognized bullama of his own ward of the village and the office will be passed on to his heirs.

The Village Area

The village area in Bornu includes a major settlement which gives the area its name and a set of surrounding smaller hamlets that are included within the political boundaries of the village area. Thus Magumeri village area includes the village of Magumeri and a series of little hamlets in the surrounding countryside. As we have seen, smaller villages are divided into wards under bullama and the hamlets surrounding the village each have their own bullama as well. In other words all recognized political leaders under a village area head are called bullama. The head of a village area, that is, the political superior of all bullamas in the village area is called the *lawan*. However the system is flexible and a few large cities such as the capital city of Maiduguri, as well as several other centers with populations over 10,000, have several lawan, each in his own ward of the city. Under these city lawan are sub-wards again under the bullama. Thus the traditional nineteenth-century system of a flexible hierarchy described in Chapter 2 in which the number and authority of political offices can expand with the settlement size is still recognized and practiced.

In Magumeri village area one lawan is responsible for the administration of the entire area. All permanent residents in the area, when asked who their local leader is, reply, "We are the commoners of Lawan Mina. We are his people." This does not apply, or at least applies less, to those persons who live locally and are themselves higher in the political hierarchy than lawan or are local representatives of the emirate civil service departments. They have their own political superiors and are responsible to others besides the lawan. Thus they give their taxes to lawan because they live in Magumeri, and he must collect the village tax, but a dispute between one of these men and a peasant would be adjudicated at a higher level in the political hierarchy than that held by lawan.

In his own part of town the lawan acts as his own ward head. Many of the compounds in the ward are reserved for his own followers, In Magumeri this includes the lawan's own compound with his four wives, married son and grandchildren, several clients and his aged mother. Some twenty followers consider themselves the active supporters of lawan under his chief follower or *wakil*. Each of these men have their own compounds near that of lawan or at least in his ward. They receive economic aid from him in the form of food, clothing, and money as well as a recognized role as a member of his retinue. Peasants often ask one of these followers to intercede with the lawan on their behalf, or to help in arranging a meeting between parties to a dispute with the lawan as the judge.

This retinue of followers who are called collectively by a special name (*waladi*) are linked together under the lawan and serve as his administrative staff. They keep in touch with gossip, aid in collecting taxes, act as contact men for anyone wishing to see him, help him on his farm plots, and carry messages for him. When he travels, several of these men are always with him on horse and on foot, and give him the appearance of being what he is—a man a cut above the common citizenry of the village area—a local official of the kingdom whose title is conferred officially by the Shehu himself. Indeed today his is the lowest rung of the political hierarchy that is recognized as a salaried job in the emirate.

This entire administrative organization of the lawan can easily be discerned by asking the people of his ward whether they would move to another village if he were transferred or dismissed. There are quite a large number in the ward who would remain. These are not his followers but they do regard him as the leader of their ward and like everyone else in the emirate they see him as the official leader of their village area. They have seen several lawans come and go, and if this particular lawan were to continually overstep the limits of his authority, they would not be averse to making some complaints about him to his superiors. Thus their good will and support must be solicited by the lawan. Indeed such a check on his authority applies to all the people in the village area. Another check which any person in the area has over the lawan is the possibility of migration. Any person is free to move away from the village area into another whenever he wishes, and a serious migration out of some political unit weakens the leadership and is almost always interpreted as a sign of faulty administration by superiors in the emirate government.

The lawan's son in Magumeri, like many others whose fathers have positions of authority, wisely avoids any active leadership in his father's administration. His job as the adult education organizer for a literary campaign in the entire district keeps him traveling much of the time, and he never interferes with the political organization which he may one day inherit. His father, on the other hand, is one of the few enthusiastic supporters of adult education and enforces the program vigorously in Magumeri since he knows this will help his son's career in the Bornu emirate government. If and when the son should ever replace his father, or gain some political office elsewhere in the kingdom, he would recruit many of his subordinates from the households of his father's followers. Thus superior-subordinate relations are often continued down the generations. Some fall by the wayside because there are always more potential followers available than needed, as the households of followers expand with their own children and clients. However since the son may choose any one within or beyond his father's administration he can insist on only the best performance and the most loyalty from those chosen. On the other hand, should the son not obtain his father's position, and not succeed in any other way in the political or economic life of Bornu, then his father's followers will begin to see that they must find places elsewhere for the younger members of their own households. When this happens the continuity of lawan's administration down the generations begins to disintegrate. This process is repeated at every level of the political hierarchy and lies near the core of political life in Bornu.

On a day-to-day basis the most important matters, especially in rural areas like Magumeri, are taken to the lawan. As we have seen in Chapter 5 he is a central figure in transferring land, using his office as a sort of registry for local land negotiations. He witnesses many marriages and divorces, and arbitrates disputes among those under his jurisdiction. Indeed most of the people living in Magumeri feel more secure about a decision they have made that might affect their neighbors if the matter is ratified and witnessed by a person in authority. Thus if a man in Magumeri village wishes to move his compound walls and expand his dwelling space, he speaks to his ward head about it, and they both go to the lawan to report the intended action. The lawan asks one or two of his followers to find out if the contiguous neighbors object, and if so on what grounds. If there is no objection the action is ratified; if some are forthcoming, then a judicial hearing results in which the lawan hears the case. What this means is that for almost everyone in Bornu, especially in the rural areas, an enormous number of everyday activities are taken through the political system when relations between households are at issue. This in turn means that the political system is close to and very involved with the daily lives of the people.

As a salaried official of the emirate government, the lawan collects taxes from all men over eighteen in the village area. This is based on property assessments of their capital in cash and kind for that particular year. Over-taxing is common in rural areas where the people are illiterate, and even when it is not done, the taxpayers believe it is common. If the over-taxing is too burdensome, it is known that complaints against the lawan to higher officials in Bornu can bring at least an investigation and perhaps lead to his dismissal.

There is no doubt that the lawan can punish people for not recognizing his authority. It is this kind of knowledge that make people aware that they must be sensitive to customary demands made of them by a lawan which if not complied with could bring punitive actions from his use of authority. Let me illustrate this by summarizing an interesting case from field notes:

Bukar is a newcomer to Magumeri. He has been given some land by the lawan and when not farming plies his trade as a hat-maker, and mud house builder. Because he had no previous social ties in the village he has attached himself to the Arabic teacher of the primary school who is a highly respected religious practitioner. This attachment appeals to Bukar because of his strong personal fears of supernatural malevolence. The Arabic teacher gives Bukar a place in the social relations of the village, plus free charms and medicines for illness and bad luck. Bukar looks after the teacher's house, repairs it, cleans it up periodically, and watches it during the latter's absence.

On one of these occasions during the teacher's absence Bukar borrowed some matting from his mentor for use within his own compound. The lawan in whose house there was to be a naming ceremony needed some extra mats for temporary shelters. He sent a follower over to the Arab teacher's compound to borrow some of the extra mats that were stocked there. These were taken, and Bukar was asked what had become of the rest of the mats. Bukar answered that he had borrowed them and that he was in charge of watching the teacher's possessions during the latter's absence. He refused to produce the matting in his own compound and was brought to the lawan where his defiance was rewarded by the lawan telling him that unless he produced the extra matting so that they could be borrowed by the lawan, then he (Bukar) was no better than a common thief. Bukar still refused and the matter was dropped.

When the teacher returned, the lawan complained to him of the disobedience and lack of respect of his man, Bukar. The teacher said nothing, but instead of reprimanding Bukar sent him to fetch back the mats borrowed by the lawan (the ceremony was now over). In so doing he indicated his support of his client, Bukar, against his fellow upperclass member in the town, namely the lawan.

Several months later Bukar was involved in a case against a Fulani nomad herdsman whose cows had strayed into one of his farm plots and eaten his millet. The case came before the lawan who ruled that, although the Fulani had pulled a knife on Bukar (a serious offense requiring a fine), it was Bukar who had started the fight, and it was this act that had caused the cow to wander over Bukar's field and devour his as well as another man's crops, besides causing the argument which made the Fulani pull a knife. Bukar was then fined heavily for starting a fight, fined for the other man's crops, and given an extra fine of five shillings which was to be paid to the district head. Bukar reports that his crops were already eaten before the fight started and besides this he and everyone else knows that pulling a knife during a fight is a separate offense from the fight itself and must be treated as such in court, and the Fulani was not fined for this misdemeanor.

In discussing the matter Bukar's senior, the teacher, explained that lawan was angry at Bukar for his behavior over the mats and was adjudicating against him for this reason. When Bukar finally raised the money for the fine, he was told by the teacher to give the money to the lawan and to say that he, Bukar, was a small, insignificant, poor peasant. He was further instructed to tell the lawan that if there was any help that the lawan needed in house building, he (Bukar) would be pleased to offer his services. The teacher also cautioned Bukar about the future.

If the lawan continued to adjudicate against him and gave him heavy fines, then he should request to take the case to a higher court. Thus the teacher wished his peasant-follower to make his peace with the lawan but if this were impossible, then higher authorities would be resorted to and the lawan's power bypassed. In other words the teacher felt that the political structure of the town should be respected but within limits.

Bukar's problem illustrates how a lawan can make reprisals when he feels that there has been some lack of recognition given to his authority by those under his administration. There are a large number of things in land matters, general disputes, ceremonials, divorces, default of bad debts, assault, housing, and commerce that come within his perview and intersect the lives of his people at a great many points and in many vulnerable ways. Therefore to thwart his authority and then remain within the orbit of his power without the possibility of reprisals would be impossible.

Recruitment to the office of the lawan is officially carried out by appointment from the emirate government at the capital. There is an official investiture ceremony at the capital, as in the nineteenth century, in which the lawan receives a turban from the Shehu of Bornu. In general there is a tendency, but only a tendency, for lawans to inherit the position. Thus one of the male heirs of the lawan takes over his household site and becomes the new lawan after his death. A male heir can be anyone in the male line of the lawan although sons seem to be favored. On the other hand many of the village areas have a history in which the office has gone to a number of men based on their particular relationship to the district head, the immediate superior of the lawan in the political hierarchy. Thus there is also a tendency for the lawan to be appointed from the ranks of the incumbent district head's followers so that the office also tends to shift from one agnatic descent group to another in relation to shifts in the person of the district head.

One other factor is important in the succession to a lawan's office. This has to do with the political allegiance of the lawan in the political hierarchy of Bornu emirate. If a lawan dies, or is dismissed, and he is not friendly to a new district head, then whether or not the district head attempts to replace him depends (a) on what are the lawan's political connections beyond that of his official superior, the district head, and (b) whether the new district head can procure the loyalty of the lawan and therefore enlist him into his own following. If a lawan has very powerful friends in the emirate, then the new district head could incur their wrath by getting the lawan out of office. A lawan is removed from his village area headship for a number of reasons although they can all be subsumed under three broad categories. First the political maneuverings of a district head who wishes to replace the lawan with his own followers. Secondly, excessive migration out of the village area, or complaints to higher officials by the peasants against the lawan, and thirdly, failure to raise enough taxes. These may, of course, be interrelated so that, for example, migration out of the village area would be spotted in the tax returns or by complaints resulting from the lawan's plan to cover up by taxing those who remain more than is bearable, thus bringing on complaints. However, if a lawan is responsive to his superiors, and does not mulct his peasants to the point of hardship, migration, and complaint, he has a fairly secure position in the Bornu political system.

The District Organization

In Bornu the lawan represents a link between the higher political authorities and the ordinary peasant. To the people in the rural areas he is the most apparent and easily reached member of the ruling classes. Their hamlet and ward heads are leaders but only in a local sense, while the lawan represents the authority of the central emirate government since he is officially appointed by this body. To many ordinary villagers the exact nature of the political organization above the level of the lawan is not at all clear. They know that beyond the lawan there is the district head and above him the Shehu of Bornu, but the various councils and agencies of the emirate government are things they know very little about in detail.

In terms of the emirate as a whole, however, the district head and his organization of the district is the pivotal political focus in Bornu. His is the office through which all central government policies from the capital are translated into action at the local level. Conversely, if there are any disturbances, irregularities in tax revenues, increases in crime, migration out of the district, or failure in any policy goals or action programs, it is to the district head that all the agencies at the center turn for an explanation.

To the lowly peasant the district head is a man in another world, a world of awesome power, riches, and courtly life. A lawan may go abroad to oversee a new well in one of his hamlets, or to mark off the boundaries of a new farm plot, or to take a tax census, but the district head rarely ever leaves his compound except for the occasional trip to oversee nomad cattle taxation, or to appear in some local ceremonial, or to attend the Shehu's court in the capital. When he does venture forth, it is a royal sally to the playing of pipes and drums, with a troop of galloping horsemen and servants brandishing swords, spears, and muzzle-loading guns. Today this is being changed somewhat by the motorcar which carries the district head quickly and silently, but district heads can still create quite a stir when they wish to go forth officially among the people.

The district organization is basically quite simple. Each of the twenty-one districts in the emirate is identified by the name of its principal village (in some cases these are quite large towns), and this latter serves as the district capital. In this capital lives the district head and his followers and all the district representatives of the various emirate civil service agencies. These include such installations as a district courthouse for the Alkali (judge) and a primary school formerly up to the end of Standard IV, now almost universally up to secondary school entrance. Formally, the district head is responsible for the administration of all the village areas and any nomadic population that may be living within the confines of the district.

The district head is appointed and installed by the Shehu in consultation with his council and the local representatives of the Northern Nigerian government. Only high ranking men in the state are considered and almost all the present district heads are sons of men who held a similar position. There is a growing tendency to try to get men who have some western education, but as yet many of the present district heads speak no English and have not attended western schools. In general, the Shehu must feel he has gained a loyal supporter and any suspicion to the contrary would bar an eligible contender from the position. The same applies in the case of members of the Shehu's council and especially its chairman, the Waziri. People say that would-be applicants give gifts, attempt to link themselves by marriage, and in general ingratiate themselves with the Shehu and his councilors who play the major part in such decisions; however such things are not easy to observe directly. On the other hand several people have told me that they regularly visit influential men in the city bringing gifts of cash and foodstuff and generally paying their respects to these men in the hopes that one day when a proper vacancy occurs, they will obtain the office of lawan. In other words this traditional mode of soliciting an appointment is admitted to for the office of lawan.

In the district capital the district head's house is always at the east end of the town plaza and is the most impressive compound in the village. The compound is regarded as emirate property and can only be used while the incumbent is in office after which time he must move out. In addition each district head has his own compound in the royal ward of Maiduguri in the capital with a residing chief subordinate (*wakil*) who appears at official state functions in the Shehu's court to represent his superior. In his rural area the district head has a large group of followers who live in his own compound and the surrounding vicinity. These men form a group of linked households under their leader, the chief follower of the district head who serves as his deputy in the latter's absence. In Magumeri a few of these followers have been recruited during their own lifetime, but most of them are the sons of men who have always been followers of this district head and his father before him.

At first glance these followers are indistinguishable from ordinary peasants except for the fact that some of them have expensive looking horses given to them by the district head. They help collect nomad cattle taxes, run messages for the district head, and never fail to ride in honor of their leader on special ceremonial occasions or when an important visitor has come to town. Most important they must be willing to leave town or move to another place whenever their superior is stationed elsewhere, while peasants are most often linked by social relations with a particular spot. These men have only one allegiance—that of subordination, discipline and respect to their superior, the district head. Thus they are never fully trusted by the more permanent local residents. Indeed younger members of the district head's following are often feared as well as mistrusted. They have no farms, no wives, and no households of their own. They talk, play cards, drink, look for amorous experiences in the local area, and are felt to be spies for the district head. When such men approach a group of peasant menfolk, the conversation suddenly stops, then slowly begins again on a note of pleasant but iridescent chit-chat in which nothing really serious or informative about local affairs is ever mentioned. Although the hierarchy of lawan and bullama under a district head is his official administrative organization in the district, his followers form an unofficial organization to execute his policies. Unlike the lawan and bullama they are totally dependent upon him for support and status in the society. In return they give him the prestige that comes from having a large retinue of followers. They also organize his tax collections, act as messengers, and sometimes they are even used to discipline lawans who are not complying with administration demands. Thus one lawan complained to a district head that he could not raise the tax assessment for his village area. The district head sent out his followers who gathered about fifty percent more than the original assessment and the lawan was then chastised and sent back with the warning that he must comply in the future with directives from the district head.

District heads' followers are outside the usual jurisdiction of those lower in the hierarchy such as the lawan. When they must be disciplined, or brought to court, they go directly to the district head or less often to the district judge by-passing the judicial authority of the lawan. Peasants seeking retribution for bad debts, adultery, or some other malfeasance committed by a district head's follower must then take the matter before the district head. This is the test of a district head's justice, and often he forces his followers to repay bad debts or fines, even though he himself is probably the one who will eventually pay the fine by advancing the money to his follower. In one case a district head publicly reprimanded one of his followers, paid his fine, then privately threatened to stop supporting this follower as his client for having burnt down a peasant's hut while drunk when the peasant refused to allow his wife to be molested by the follower. A district head who continually protects his own followers against the peasants develops a reputation as a tyrant and an inefficient administrator. Given the present government it is difficult to hide bad administration since complaints by peasants to touring officials usually provide information to people higher up in the political organization concerning the activities of a district head and his organization.

As suggested above there is sometimes a strain in the relations between a district head and the various lawans who head up the village areas within the district. Formally he relays directives from the capital to them in their village areas and they are supposed to carry out these policies. However the district head needs cooperation, often for necessary but somewhat semi-illicit activities and thus needs people he can trust in leadership positions within the district. On his side the lawan is semi-independent because he is a salaried official. District heads are constantly trying to win the affection and loyalty of their lawans, or if necessary to get them expelled, or wait until they retire and then have the office filled by one of their own loyal followers. Because district heads are constantly being retired, dismissed, or transferred from one district to another, each new district head is confronted with a number of lawans who are the loyal followers of predecessors who were district heads in the area.

The records of turnover of lawans, especially in the district capital, where they must see the district head continually, show that in general lawans are dismissed or retired most often shortly after the arrival of a new district head. The case of one lawan in Magumeri illustrates this very common occurrence. From 1921 to 1929 a lawan in Magumeri village area was a follower of the district head of Magumeri District. In 1929 a new district head arrived and suddenly the quality of reports by colonial officials changed. Whereas before this man was reported to be cooperative, intelligent, hard-working, and competent, he was now unpopular with the people, there was much emigration from his village area due to heavy taxation, and he was disrespectful to those in authority. In 1933 he was suspended by the Shehu, and a younger brother of the new district head was appointed to the lawan's office for the Magumeri village area. Examples like this are extremely common in the history of all the districts right up to the present time.

As in the example above there is a tendency for the district heads to appoint younger brothers to the post of lawan within their own districts. However this has its limits. In one case a lawan confidentially asked the British officials if he could be moved to a district away from the hegemony of his older brother, the district head. That same year (1935) there were a great many complaints by the peasants directed to British officials about the harshness of this particular district head's administration. He was warned but did not comply and was later dismissed. The younger brother sensed that trouble was brewing for the older brother and decided it would be more advantageous to his own career if he could move to another district and not get caught up in the difficulties his brother was creating by his lack of good administration. One district head remarked that he had tried to appoint his own brother in a previous district as lawan, but the young man had done a very bad job and it proved impossible for the district head to control him. The younger brother was finally deposed by the emirate government after his older brother was transferred to a new district. Later he came to his older brother in the latter's new district, hoping for another job as lawan in his brother's administration. However the older brother has no intention of doing so because, as he says, this younger brother is a bad man who oppresses his villagers when he gets a chance and this reflects back on the district head. Thus in Bornu the loyalty of brothers is ameliorated in the political system by the requirements of office.

As we have already noted, local representatives of the various Bornu Native Authority (emirate government) departments are stationed in the district capitals. These include people like the district chief scribe who keeps the books on revenue collection, the district judge, the school teachers, some native authority policemen, veterinary, forestry, and agricultural department representatives and so on. The list varies in length from district to district, but there is a general tendency for it to lengthen through time as the departments expand their programs and services. These officials are paid salaries and live in the district capital although they often get shifted from one district to another. Thus only one of these officials in Magumeri had been there for longer than four years and almost all of them had lived in at least three district capitals during the past ten years. They view themselves as a class apart from the local people; they are city bred or at least city educated; they share a common interest in state and national politics; and their mobility orients them to each other rather than to people outside the civil service. When asked who their best friends are they invariably mention other members of the emirate's civil service. Thus they form a class of urban cosmopolitans on the rural scene.

Their relations to the district head are complex and in some ways similar to that of the district head to his lawans when these latter are appointees of a previous district head. The native authority official is not necessarily a follower of the district head, and he does have a separate salary. Usually the official and the district head maintain a respectful but carefully measured social distance from one another. The local officials are often asked to eat at the compound of the district head which emphasizes their common urban upper-class membership and separateness as a group from the rural population. However, they generally do not become members of the district head's following. They have their own careers to follow, and though friendship with the district head is useful, it could also impede their success because of demands made upon them by the district head which might conflict with those of their own departmental superiors in the capital.

On the other hand the local official must work through the district head if he wishes to carry out his job successfully. Children are ordered into the district school through the district head's office. Forestry reserves are set up by his directive; cattle are rounded up by him. Indeed almost any action involving a response by the people in the district must come originally from the district head. A lawan, if approached for cooperation by civil service employees, would generally refuse to cooperate if he had not been first notified by the district head's office. The district head is a high official of the state while the native authority employee is generally the lowest status field representative of his department. Thus they pay the district head respect, stand up when he approaches them, take off their shoes before entering his compound, and consult him on programs they wish to have carried out in his district.

On his part the district head quickly establishes who the native authority officials are, and what families they come from or are connected to in the emirate. If the district head is closely connected by friendship and political alliance to a high-placed official in the local representative's department, then he may have an avenue of control over this local person through the latter's own superior. On the other hand the native authority employee may be connected with the powerful people in the emirate and the district head then knows that this particular official could possibly bring powerful forces into action if a situation warranted it.

The relationships of the district head to the capital are highly complex and result from the fact that he is the official link between the central government of the emirate and the local political organization of the district. Officially he is responsible to only one body, the central agency of the emirate government which is the Shehu-in-Council. This council, called the Bornu Native Authority Council, under the chairmanship of the Waziri or chief minister, is the highest authority in the emirate. As we noted in Chapter 2, the council acts like a cabinet and each member has a Native Authority department under his direction. District heads receive instructions about policy from the council and directives about programs from each of the departments. The district head delivers taxes to the Native Authority Treasury and must account for his actions to the council which has a major voice in appointing, dismissing, retiring, and transferring district heads from high to low-paying districts or vice versa.

Both during the colonial period and at the present, the Bornu Provincial Government has had several emirates under its jurisdiction, of which Bornu is the largest. Although not officially responsible to the Provincial Government, the district head and his work have always been inspected periodically by touring officers of the Provincial Government. These men can make recommendations which influence the emirate government and during colonial times there are a number of records of district heads being retired or dismissed because of the "advice" of Provincial Government officials. Thus the district head has to be sure his actions are in line with the demands and standards of provincial officials who are today generally from other parts of Northern Nigeria, and were, up to a few years ago, the British colonial officers.

The district head has other links with the capital as well. As we have already noted, he keeps a household in the palace ward of the capital city, and his followers in his compound under a wakil, or chief follower, visit the palace regularly as his representatives. The wakil also makes regular visits to important emirate leaders and tries to maintain a constant check on political developments in the capital and the emirate as a whole. Through this organization and through the giving of gifts and hospitality to visitors and messengers from the capital, as well as cultivating high placed friends, the district head maintains and builds up a communication network through which he obtains a many-sided picture of events in the capital.

District heads are also linked to the capital by their membership in factions that help to make up the political life of the emirate. In pre-colonial times these factions grew out of the allegiance of nobles to the various segments of the royal lineage. This indeed was the reason the succession disputes to the throne could turn into bloody civil wars. These same traditional factions still exist today, but there have been added new ones which involve close alliances between very powerful men in the emirate government. These reflect the weakened authority of the Shehu, and the increase in power and authority of the Native Authority officials in the top positions of the emirate government. District heads linked to more powerful factions receive better information about the course of emirate politics and more protection when they need it than those related to weak ones. Thus one district head might be linked to a member of the royal family who has no official position in the Native Authority and who has little hope of gaining the throne; another might be closely linked to the Waziri or chairman of the Bornu Native Authority Council. The latter district head, because of his factional membership, is in a much stronger position in the emirate political organization as a whole than is the former. These links to the center both official and unofficial must be carefully developed and maintained by a district head. This is especially true when it is realized that a district head like any other member of the Bornu political system operates within two cultural orientations—one western and the other traditional Kanuri. The district head should give gifts to subordinates, to his faction leaders, and to many other powerful people in the state. From a western point of view these can be seen as bribes, while from a Kanuri vantage point they may be looked upon as obligatory and legitimate recognition by the district head of the power and protection that can be wielded by his superiors in the central government of the emirate. Since such expenses are not provided for in the district head's official salary, the means by which he obtains the wealth to make such gifts often involves breaking rules according to strict western civil service standards, although again such activities might be considered legitimate by local tradition.

The central focus of this behavior revolves around tax collection. The district head is seen in western terms to be an agent of government who collects taxes and is paid a salary for this and other services. However, he needs to maintain a large following who are not provided for by government if he is going to collect nomad cattle taxes. These men must ride out over the entire district—often several thousand square miles—to collect the tax. To keep these men as his tax collectors he needs much more revenue than his own salary. If he does not collect the tax, or enough taxes, he will be punished by dismissal or transfer to a smaller less prestigious district. He has very little choice; in order to keep his own organization going and to maintain friendly contact at the center by gift-giving, he must take some of the district's tax revenue for himself. This makes him vulnerable at all times; to comply with some demands which are deemed important he must break others which he hopes are less important. Furthermore, as in any bureaucracy, standards and their enforcement change through time, often as a result of changing personnel at the top. A new council member may have become interested in school latrines and suddenly start forcing compliance with the rules about such things. Failure to do so or to hear about the stringency with which the old previously unimportant policies are now being enforced could bring trouble to the district head who failed to comply. This is why information about policy and the cultivation of powerful friends in the central government is so important for the district head.

Before leaving the rural area a word should be said about adjudication. All leaders in the Bornu political system adjudicate disputes, and the political hierarchy itself serves as an appeals court system. Thus a peasant can take his dispute with a neighbor to his bullama (hamlet or ward head), who may decide to take the case up to the lawan (village area head), who in turn may decide to take the case to the district head. The district head may further decide to send the case over to the district court, and, if necessary, the district court can send the case into the capital city, to the court of the chief alkali of Bornu (chief judge's court). People can go directly to the judge's or district court, and in the city many do. Even with very serious cases like murder which must go into the central court in the city, the people taking the murderer into the city court most often go up the political hierarchy reporting the case each time they see another official even though there is no adjudication, thus giving recognition to their political leaders rather than going directly to a higher court.

Cases are tried by a combination of Muslim law and local custom. The chief or judge listens to the case, and if three witnesses swear for one side in a dispute but not the other, then the side whose witness has sworn wins the case. If no one swears evidence or too many people swear on both sides, then the judge listens while his assistant in the court interrogates the parties involved. The judge, whoever he may be, then makes a decision. Very often the interrogation itself tends to move the evidence towards one side in a dispute or another. Usually if a crowd gathers, one can see by simply listening to the crowd which side of the court case is winning the argument. On the whole decisions are just unless there have been previous and difficult relations between the adjudicator and any of the parties concerned. Swearing evidence in a court is called "eating the Koran"; that is to say, a person must swear on the holy book. If he tells a lie, it is believed that his hand will shrivel and he will die of horrible diseases. This belief is widespread and it is genuinely feared that the traditionally implied consequences of lying in court are in fact quite true.

The Organization at the Center

In Maiduguri at the eastern end of the royal plaza is the palace of the Shehu, flanked on one side by the mosque and on the other by the official residence of the Waziri or chief minister of the emirate. The Shehu is the formal head of government. All measures, policies, appointments, made within the state are in his name; titles are granted at official investiture ceremonies carried on in the royal palace and he is the formal leader of the religious community of the state. This is embodied in his title, "commander of the faithful," and is expressed ritually in a number of ways. Thus at the feast celebrating the end of Ramadan (the annual Muslim fast), a special ram of the Shehu is killed by the chief religious leader of the state. No one considering himself a citizen of the emirate and a subject of the Shehu is supposed to kill his own ram for the feast day until the royal ceremony is completed.

At all annual festivals and state occasions, and every Friday to a lesser extent, the Shehu is attended at his palace by his court and representatives of the people. The court includes members of the royal family, title holders, the Native Authority council members, and any district heads who may be in the capital or their city representatives who sit outside the royal courtroom. Into the royal presence come representatives of each Native Authority department, representatives of the religious leaders of the community, a sample of school children, leaders and representatives of the various occupational groupings under their own headmen. Each group gives symbolic pledges of loyalty and obedience to the throne by saying prayers for the health and welfare of the monarch and the state. The people, including the nobles, go down on their knees to the monarch, stand when he stands, remove their shoes in his presence, and speak to him only indirectly using terms of reverence and respect.

It is difficult to assess what real power the Shehu has in the emirate government. The present incumbent is a very old man, and for the last decade or so the bulk of administrative affairs have been handled by the Native Authority Council under the direction of the Waziri. Whether this now indicates a trend toward constitutional monarchy or whether a new, younger and more vigorous Shehu would reassert the power of the throne is a question that is fascinating but at present not capable of being answered. Certainly the Native Authority Council and the various departments under the council are new and growing powers in the contemporary society, but the district heads are formally responsible to the Shehu. Since the district heads are still very powerful members of the political system, a new Shehu could conceivably affect policy and the administration of the emirate very considerably through his influence on these men and their appointments. It is also very possible that he would influence the Native Authority Council itself and appointments to that body. Potentially the office is a very powerful one, and it seems unlikely that its power will diminish in future since the instruments of power are available to anyone occupying the throne who wishes to use them.

The main business of government of the emirate is handled on a day-to-day basis in the Native Authority departments, which are coordinated with similar departments in other emirates of the province under the Bornu Provincial Government which in its turn looks to the Regional Government of Northern Nigeria for policy directives that are regional in scope.

The personnel of the Native Authority departments form what has come to be called a new class in the society. They are salaried bureaucrats who work in offices and generally have some form of western education. They wear wrist watches, read English and vernacular newspapers, listen to the radio for both local, national, and international news, go to political meetings, join civil service associations, and think of themselves as urban even when they are stationed in the rural areas. Their goals are almost universally to obtain more qualifications and to advance in the civil service to higher paid jobs with more authority and prestige.

Recruitment into the departments can be carried out in a variety of ways. An application can be sent to the Native Authority Council or the relevant departments in writing. People seem to think this is not an effective way of obtaining a position, and it is rarely practiced. Another way is to obtain new recruits from among the school graduates of the secondary schools. This is becoming more and more common as time goes on, however it is a highly impersonal technique and thus not attractive to many in the community who still feel that they must have some private, personal relationship with their superiors-to-be before they can obtain any rewards for themselves. Thus it is widely believed that such personal relationships are the primary requisite to enlistment in the civil service, given that the educational qualifications are satisfactory. Thus one young man working in the Native Authority civil service explained it this way:

> If you want a job in the . . . department, one of your relatives should find the name of a person in the department who is known to help people. Your relative then goes to greet him in the evening and gives him some money and perhaps other gifts. The man who can help then tells your relative to come back at such and such a time and he will let him know the result. Then he will try to find a job in the department, probably by using some of the money your relative gave him. Then the job is yours and you are an employee of the Native Authority . . . sometimes it takes a long time.

Certainly young boys with higher educational qualifications have less difficulty obtaining jobs, but as the educational system increases the numbers of its graduates at upper levels, then places in the Native Authority will become less available, and so this particular method of recruitment will in all likelihood remain for some time to come.

The emirate civil service departments have two standards that employees must maintain at all costs. First, they must be competent at their job, and the leaders of the emirate are always interested in raising such levels. Job re-training schemes, and trips by senior department members to other parts of Nigeria or even overseas are becoming more and more common. Secondly, there must be loyalty and obedience to the department. This is traditional and involves the same kind of behavior we have observed in all community relationships involving superiors and subordinates, starting with the household and moving out into the society as a whole. However departments are too large for very intimate contacts and some of the impersonality of modern bureaucracy has entered to make relations somewhat unpredictable. One young man complained that in his department it is essential to dress less well than one's superior or one would be considered overly ambitious, threatening, and untrustworthy. On the other hand it is also important not to dress too poorly or people in authority would consider one a wastrel who spends his money on women, praise-singers, and drink. Again it is, according to many of the younger men, difficult to transfer from one department to another. To transfer, a formal application must be made to one's own department superiors and to the Native Authority Council; if a release is granted, then a further application to some other department can be submitted. Those reporting this procedure said it was practically impossible since it meant rejecting your own superiors, not your job, and it would be similar to someone in a household saying he was fed up when he decided to leave. Thus in Kanuri cultural terms, changing a job means rejecting the people with whom one works, and young men claim they would be considered ingrates and trouble-makers if they were to attempt such a thing. Transfers, if they are to be accomplished at all, must be done through relatives and friends who can "visit at night" with the appropriate people and explain the ins and outs of the case so that things can be arranged on this personal basis first before any impersonal bureaucratic procedures are utilized.

On the surface the emirate civil service looks very westernized. There are offices, typewriters, clerks, officials, expense vouchers, committees, memoranda, telephones, employee organizations, etc. However within the service, traditional patterns of association are still very strongly observed. A man lifts the telephone and traditional greetings and modes of address to a superior flow forth and color the conversation. People leave their shoes outside a superior's office, and so on. Under these superficial cultural acts there are other things as well. "Big men" (senior officials) have large compounds linked to a number of clients who live either in their households or close by. Some of these subordinates have positions in the civil service. Others form part of this big man's own group of followers; he must be approached through this group and he uses it to maintain his position and prestige in the state. It is also important to understand that the western concept of loyalty to an ideal of public service is not widespread as yet. Top leaders are committed to the maintenance of order in a just society that is becoming more modern. Within the Native Authority, department loyalties are to one's superiors and personal advancement is through loyalty and generalized obedience, just as it always has been in Kanuri society, and not to an abstract ideal of public service and bureaucratic efficiency. This does not mean that rationalized bureaucratic behavior will not become more common in Bornu. Indeed everything we know about modernization suggests that this is inevitable. However, it does mean that at present the society is not divided into strict sectors, one labelled modern or western, the other traditional. Instead, each of these permeates the other so that everything new and modern is shot through with traditional culture, and everything traditional has aspects of the modern.

Representative Government

For most intents and purposes the political organization of the emirate is carried out within the system of offices and agencies described above. However there are today the bare bones of some other kinds of organization that are quite likely to prove important in the future. During the 1950s and continuing on to the present time, each district has had a local district council. This body is made up of members from all over the district, sometimes the village area heads, sometimes people appointed by them. They meet only a few times a year for one or two days under the chairmanship of the district head and discuss local affairs. These meetings are generally attended as well by members of the departments of local government from the capital. The councils have a budget based on a small proportion of the taxes raised in the district and they meet primarily to discuss the dispensation of these funds. Usually this has to do with items of local improvement such as market stalls in various villages in the district, radios for hamlets and villages, etc. They also draft resolutions asking the emirate government for help in extending roads, building wells, and so on.

The official representative from the capital—previously from the colonial government, now the local government department of the emirate—who attends the meetings provides a link between this group and the central government in Maiduguri. He advises them on what is and what is not feasible in terms of their requests to the central government and also informs them of long-range development policies and plans by the central emirate government.

So far these councils are quite weak. They meet only a few times a year and have a very limited function. However as time goes on they could assume the role of a local legislative and administrative body made up of people who represent the developing needs of ordinary people to participate in decisions affecting their own local areas.

During the last decade or so another form of political activity has come to Bornu in the form of political parties. The traditional authorities, the district heads, lawans, judges, officials of the Native Authority, and all their followers, support the N.P.C. (Northern Peoples Congress) which represents similar interests in other parts of Northern Nigeria and forms the dominant element in the federal government of Nigeria. Several days a week in various parts of Maiduguri, but only rarely in rural areas, public meetings are held under the green flag of the N.P.C. Meetings are usually preceded by drumming and traditional dancing by divorced women. Then party organizers make speeches to the assembled crowds. Sometimes the "big men" such as the district heads or Native Authority Councilors attend these meetings especially around election time, but they themselves and candidates for office do not speak. To do so is considered demeaning for the "big men." Instead party organizers give long, loud harangues extolling the virtues of the N.P.C. and go into great detail about the evils propagated by other political parties in Nigeria.

The overall effect of these political meetings is one of tradition versus its breakdown, good versus evil, ethnic and religious unity and loyalty versus disunity and disloyalty. The real, everyday authority in the lives of the people obviously supports the N.P.C. Thus a vote against this party means much more than a simple political decision to support one contending group of leaders against another; it means that the person is turning against the traditional political structure of the society, and by inference that moral order that holds it together. Listeners at the meetings are constantly presented with moral choices; "are you against our own chiefs, the district heads, lawans, our Shehu?—well *they,* the opposition parties, are; are you against wives being obedient to their husbands?—well *they* are; are you against children being obedient to their parents?—well *they* are," and so on. Stories are told of people whose parents were fine and upstanding citizens who supported and were supported by their leaders. Then their children ran away and supported opposition parties having first rejected the authority, love, affection and support of their own parents. Such people are now vagrants with no families, no proper connections to a respectable Kanuri household, no place in society, and no proper place in the social and moral life of the community. It is prophesied that morality and family life as it is now known could be destroyed if opposition parties ever came to power. Finally, it is always pointed out that opposition parties represent the Southern Nigerians and that a vote for such a group is a vote against Islam, the true religion, and a vote for paganism covered by a thin cloak of Christianity.

During the 1950s when there was an active local opposition party in Bornu under a Kanuri leader, attitudes to the opposition were more clearly seen. The British colonial officials dealt mostly with senior Kanuri members of the Native Authority. Both the British and these Kanuri leaders had an abhorrence of disorder, riots, or activities that could lead to such disturbances. It was thought that allowing Southern Nigerians to organize branches of their own party locally was one thing but having a Kanuri opposition party was quite another. Events proved them correct, for in 1958 riots broke out in Maiduguri between supporters of the N.P.C. and the Bornu Youth League. The ins and outs of these riots need not concern us here, but from that time on the B.Y.L. was crushed. Many of its local leaders fled to other parts of Nigeria or to neighboring Chad to reappear several years later and eventually to become loyal N.P.C. supporters. Today although other Nigerian parties are represented in Bornu, their supporters and local organizers are all non-Kanuri. Thus the emirate government is linked to Nigerian party politics through a one-party organization which represents the traditional authority system of the emirate.

The party and its place as a dominant element in Nigerian politics means that Kanuri leaders have open to them regional and federal appointments. There are Kanuri in the federal cabinet and in the various federal ministries. Up until January 1966, the political head of the N.P.C. and the Premier of the northern region was the Sarduana of Sokoto, and the Governor was Sir Kashim Ibrahim, the former Waziri of Bornu.[1] The old nineteenth century balance of power in this region between the empires of Bornu and Sokoto still remain, then, and both must be represented in the leading positions of this, the largest region of Nigeria.

In summary, Kanuri political organization is basically structured along the lines set up by the colonial era which were built onto those of pre-colonial times. As the emirate has developed a need for more modern political structures these have appeared and are continuing to appear as the society changes towards more modernization and the accumulation of social and economic development. Within this structure modes of behavior are still largely traditional as are the values and political ideology that give the present system its immediate and long range goals. Whether or not modernism and its values will eventually produce a clash with tradition or whether the change will continue to be as smooth and incremental as it has in the past is one of the key questions for the future.

---

[1] As this is being written the politics of Nigeria, and in all probability its constitutional make-up, are being changed by the effects of the military take-over of the federal government which occurred in January, 1966.

7

Conclusion

T HIS THEN, is the Kanuri society of Bornu as I have come to know it over a period of years. I have left many things out or merely skimmed over them in order to make a major point. There is a rich ceremonial life related to the annual cycle of Islamic festivals; there are beliefs about the nature of the world, how it is constructed and what causes things to happen in it. There is a complicated set of concepts about social rank and class which I have not gone into; and there are, I believe, distinct features of personality that give to Kanuri individuals a set of attitudes that are adapted to their own way of life. Some of these I know about, others, like their personality, I only suspect but cannot as yet prove because of inadequate information. However the features that have been described were those designed to answer the question quoted at the beginning of this book. In the first Chapter I asked, "What are the set of organized activities by which the Kanuri of Bornu have adapted to their environment and created means for the maintenance, continuity, and evolution of their society?" My answer to this question has been to show how a number of different sectors of Kanuri social life are interrelated and built up from the basic unit of society, namely the household organization and the modes of behavior utilized in the household or compound in its everyday activities.

Taking this approach I have been reflecting the opinions and beliefs of my Kanuri informants. In other words, my basic theory about Kanuri society and how it operates is really not my own but that used by the Kanuri themselves when they try to explain their own society in general terms. In trying to instruct me about their culture and how it works, they continually harken back to the household. The household is the basic political unit in Bornu; groups of households link up to form wards, hamlets, villages, and districts. To found a new settlement one or more linked households move out and begin to operate as a semi-independent community. The everyday business of getting a living is organized within a household, and a series of households linked through their household heads can form larger economic organizations for productive or trading purposes. Family life, the crucible of human society, is of course centered within the household. Finally the modes of behavior that one requires in order to adapt to everyday social relationships in the society are learned within the household.

111

What about larger organizations like the emirate political hierarchy and the trading organizations based on stores or canteens, that is to say, modern business enterprises? These obviously contain people who are not members of the same household. Certainly this is true, but often, as in the trading organizations, junior clerks in the store did at one time live in the household of the store owner or still do live there. Much more important, the Kanuri claim, is the fact that the proper way to behave in a political or economic hierarchy is the way one behaves in a household organization or a set of linked households. The junior in the organization gives bər-zum (or discipline-respect) to his superior and in return he receives the benefits of membership, that is to say, he receives a social and political status, protection, and economic gain, for the loyalty and obedience which he delivers to his superior. This to the Kanuri is the most important single behavior in social life. It is learned in the household and then used to link households and individuals together in all of the organizations that are important in the society as a whole. The inference here is that the society is basically and essentially hierarchical—one in which most relationships are of a superior-subordinate variety—and indeed this is true except for friendship groups that do not, however, carry on many of the fundamental activities in Bornu.

It is because this underlying unity is still so firm and central a feature of Kanuri social life that I have not stressed the fact that my trips to Bornu straddle the historic fact of Nigerian independence. Political independence has brought no change in the way in which the bulk of the Kanuri organize their social life and live out the contents of their daily lives in their households, their villages, and their emirate. These modes of behaving have ancient roots in the area, and independence has not witnessed any widespread attempts to change things or to create new modes of organizing the social life of the emirate. Top administrators are now Nigerians, not British colonial officials, but what and how they administer in Bornu is roughly the same as it was in the pre-independence era of the 1950s. When I spoke to some of the leaders of the emirate in 1965 about their understanding of changes that might occur in the political system or the way in which the emirate was organized, they commented that the system was efficient and could serve as a stable, trustworthy form of local political organization through which any changes might come and still keep Bornu as a viable entity for a long time in Nigeria's future.

What is different today, and different only in degree, is the commitment to modernization on the part of top leadership and the initiative they are willing to show in this regard. The leaders are committed whole-heartedly to expanding western education, obtaining better health services, and decreasing disease. They also hope to increase productivity in agriculture and introduce the beginnings of industrialization into Bornu. Steps are being taken in all directions, and only the future can tell what of the past will actually enter into a future that at least on the surface seems in its ultimate goal to be so different from the majestic past and the present of the Kanuri of Bornu.

8

Epilogue, 1986

As I noted at the outset the culture and society described in this ethnography are alive and well. The large rural land area within Borno State remains populated mostly by Kanuri. Distinctive customs, a sense of pride in ancient roots, and above all the language and its daily use create a firm basis for continuity. What will happen in the future cannot be predicted with certainty, but a number of trends have become well-entrenched. The results can be reported with a high degree of confidence. First, I will briefly summarize the major events of the past twenty years highlighting continuity and change in regards to the land, the people, their economy and socio-political life.

As the Third World goes, Nigeria has been among the most blessed. In the early years of independence (1960s) oil was discovered and began delivering unimagined national wealth. With the surge in oil prices of the early 1970s even that level was surpassed many times over. Factories, roads, schools, universities, and suburbs burgeoned so that every time I visited the country during the 1960s and 1970s there were massive new developments. The first two decades of independence witnessed a true boom; it was a time of unquenchable optimism and growth. It ended abruptly at the end of the 70s and early 80s when the bottom started falling out of the oil market. Nigeria began experiencing serious financial problems: food deficits, unemployment, inflation and a population explosion. While it lasted, the boom brought enormous changes. In the cities, money was spent lavishly and was enjoyed.

Borno shared in this prosperity. Its cities and towns have grown at over 5% per year, doubling in size every 14 or 15 years. In the late 1950s when we first arrived, Maiduguri, the state capital, was a gentle town of 35,000 in the farthest corner of the country. Today it is at least ten times that size. Modern hotels, factories, a TV station, restaurants, huge state and federal office complexes, a large suburbia of fine houses and a federal university and teaching hospital are obvious differences directly related to the oil boom. A new international airport soon will be completed to link the city to the Middle East and Europe. Private sector airlines now compete with the government owned Nigerian Airways running daily discount flights to major cities. A color-coded new city market is rising out of the older one destroyed by fire in the 1970s. In colonial times,

Maiduguri was the end of the road; the most remote outpost away from Lagos, the national capital. Today the roads are paved, a train runs regularly and the national radio and TV hook-up link the city to the outside world. Morning newspapers arrive on the early plane and are hawked on the streets as the suburban office workers drive, walk, bicycle or take a bus to work. Oil wealth has transformed a quiet savannah city into a bustling metropolis.

In the back streets of the city, however, mud-walled compounds still abound. New houses and walls are generally of cement block; all roofing is corrugated metal sheeting. Clean water from pipe stands on streets is available, most houses have electricity and hundreds of small shops offer products from around the world. Inflation and recent (1980s) government foreign exchange controls intervene between supply and demand to create scarcities of consumer goods which fuel price rises.

Change also brings problems. The influx into the cities has produced housing shortages, crime and masses of underemployed men and women seeking to make a living. Hawking, begging, servicing, trying to make something to sell are commonplace. Concurrently, people are desperate to find a patron-kinsman, fellow townman, inquisitive anthropologist or anyone who might give them a start toward some gainful activity. In Maiduguri all of these issues are exacerbated by added numbers of people fleeing the civil war in Chad. One has only to walk down a city street past the halt and the blind, open sewers, and small hills of uncollected garbage to know that Maiduguri is a third world city of the late twentieth century. The rapid change has created many problems including over-population and worrisome, ever-present poverty.

Out in the rural areas there are also some troubling changes. In the far north of Borno, bits and pieces of desertification are sending ominous spurs southwards. The ancient grass-covered stationary dunes are still there telling the story of a pulsating desert that expands and contracts in response to complex forces not yet understood by science. The checkered advance of a true set of sand dunes that will transform the savannah and sahel into desolation is real and threatening in the northern parts of the state. Farther south near the city, a new nemesis is apparent. The bursting city uses fuelwood as its main source of energy for cooking. Great and small piles of firewood lie at the roadside near each village awaiting the vans and trucks that carry them to the city every day. Topsoil is fragile and loose; fuel is costly. Borno is experiencing what all more developed and rapidly growing societies must face: the degradation of its environment whether from drought, over-use, or the lack of careful and regulated conservation.

This leads to the most important caveat in the book. Although I had been apprised of the possibility and understood it intellectually, the possibility of drought did not really affect my description and analysis of Kanuri culture. The period when I first visited the area is now known to have been the wettest in decades. I made little or no point of this in the research or in the book. Later, in the early 1970s and '80s my wife and I witnessed devastating crop failures first hand. Working in Magumeri in 1984 the District Head said that only ten to fifteen miles north our hearts would break if we saw the parched fields of millet.

We went; he was right. The savannah is a marginal area on the rim of a great desert. Droughts and crop failures, lack of water and pasture for cattle, sheep, and goats have always been a regular and unpredictable feature of life. Until rural development catches up so that water management and conservation provide a safety net, the basis of rural economic life will remain at the mercy of nature. Empty granaries and real privation are spectres that haunt Kanuri life no matter how well households plan and work to feed themselves. This is the one serious oversight in the book. The extraordinary wet period of my first field work blinded me to the risky quality of savannah subsistence. Later research trips corrected the mistake, but I must acknowledge it to set the record straight.

What happens in a drought? As one would expect, households first resort to their own resources of labor and capital. Non-farm work is expanded; some members find work as farmers in wetter areas or go to the city to find employment in order to send cash back to their home village. Neighbors and kin help with food if they have it. In extreme conditions — repeated crop failures in successive years — households, related groups, or even entire small villages migrate to wetter areas. Talking to people in a drought-ridden village near Lake Chad in 1984, the Village Head told me that this was the third consecutive year of poor or failed crops. Many of the men had left town to put in a quick crop of maize and beans on the now exposed bottom of the Lake about 25 miles east of the village. He said it would probably not be enough to feed the town. There had been no help from outside nor did he expect any (for complex political reasons the village is situated in an administrative no-man's land avoided by development agencies). If the same conditions occur again next year, the village will abandon its present site and move southwards. People cope, but how well or how poorly is unknown. In extreme situations, as occurred in 1973 and 1974, urban households take on rural relatives and friends, even strangers. The strong value in Islamic religion of helping the needy relieves some of the despair. Again, how many people receive help, how many fall through the cracks and what happens to them is not well understood.

State and federal governments have been instituting programs on a national level to combat the declining per capita food supply. Special programs are in effect to increase and to modernize farm production. Water management schemes are being put into operation. Reforestation programs and road building to open remote farming communities are being developed. Future prospects are encouraging, but in the short run Borno is a vulnerable land. People are still subject to the random risk of privation over which there is no control. Hope, prayer, and the social system described in this book are the only sources of succor.

In terms of other major historical events, Borno's remoteness left it moderately untouched for the first few years of independence. The ups and downs of Nigerian politics seemed to be happening elsewhere, although as noted (pp.108-110) party politics added to the traditional authority system and supported it.

After the breakdown of the first civilian government (in 1966) events moved rapidly to bring Borno into the mainstream of Nigerian national life.

The emirate itself was dwarfed when a new entity, Northeast State was formed from three former colonial provinces. At first, there was competition. Each of the provinces wanted its own major city to be the new state capital. Maiduguri won out, but it was a pyrrhic victory. Suddenly, the city was home to hosts of strangers who came in droves to work and live in the new capital. As the major administrative center of a vast region, the city attracted traders, craftsmen, relatives, hangers-on, etc. all looking for jobs and a place on the ladder. For the first time in its modern history, the Kanuri people were a minority in their own state and in their capital town.

The city overflowed. Buildings, businesses, office complexes, housing, improved roads and services, and urban plans for the rest of the century burst into being in a few short years (1967-1974). The old town and the emirate government remained, still the very heart of Kanuri culture and tradition. The city, however, grew in all directions leaving the historic core as a respected enclave, the seat of traditional power and authority. One of the new building complexes, the Governor's Residence at the entrance to the old European residential area, is much larger, more modern and more impressive than the Shehu's palace. Times have changed.

In the midst of all these changes, the old Shehu of Borno died. In the rivalries that followed it became difficult to find a successor. The Shehu had been in office since the late 1930s. Ancient forms of decision-making no longer applied in light of the widespread changes taking place. Regional and national interests made themselves known and had to be taken into account. Borno Emirate elites were forced to realize how much a part of the larger whole they had become. After this episode, successions to the Shehuship became easier. It was now clear to all concerned that the degree of autonomy they had enjoyed before and during colonial rule was gone forever.

Even though the former province (now Borno State) has been restored, the enormous development of Maiduguri and its large administrative and business communities are essentially northern Hausa-speaking Nigerian. Practically all urban Kanuri now speak Hausa and the language is spreading rapidly into the rural areas. Parents currently teach their children Kanuri as a first language, but it is uncertain how long that will continue. Until the 1960s, non-Kanuri ethnic groups learned Kanuri because of the dominant position of this group in Borno. Today, middle-aged and older members of the non-Kanuri groups speak it fluently. Younger people in their teens and twenties use Hausa as a second language. As Nigerian nationhood congeals and integrates socially, economically, and politically, Kanuri has become another among many home languages, Hausa, English, or both are moving into dominance as national languages.

Despite all of these portentous events, Borno is clearly continuous with the place and the people depicted in my earlier study. The oil boom, the explosive growth of the capital city, the death of the Shehu, the droughts, and the civil war have signaled great changes. These have been integrated into the way of life described in this book. It is the contrasts that one sees first. Below the surface, in the households and in the lives of people we have known for many years the old pattern of life goes on. Cultures change; they adapt, absorb and persist.

The rural areas have not emptied out. A high proportion of the population has always lived in rural areas. Birth rates are high and rising in response to better health facilities. Despite migration to the city, there is a growing population on the farms. The size of the urban non-farming population has been increasing at about twice the rate of the general populace. Each farmer must thus produce more food for the growing number of non-producers. Urbanization increases the demand on farmers or the demand for imported foods.

All this aside, Borno is still predominantly rural. Villages are bigger and more farmland is under cultivation. Close-knit village life is still the rule for at least three-quarters of the population. As a result, the life described in this book goes on relatively unchanged. Although not apparent to the eye, there are proportionately more independent or semi-independent households. Nucleation, the process of setting up new households rather than increasing the size of one's family compound to accommodate new generations of extended kin, has increased from about 1/3 to 1/2 of all households. The possibility has increased that sons will develop their own farms or non-farm occupations. Nevertheless, fathers, sons and brothers still appear in court together as a group. They frequently live near one another, practice the same or related occupations, and support one another in village affairs. The extended, patrilocal, family group is alive and well whether they live under one roof or not.

Relations within households are almost identical to those described earlier. The household head makes the major decisions about when, where and what to plant. He has full control over household marketing, production, food storage, and non-farming activities. Household members often have individual activities, but they are obligated to help with household work and to accept the authority of the head. Households are still the chief holders of land; they provide the basis for occupational training, ceremonial life and the creation of an identity for individuals as persons in a community.

Farming is still essentially subsistence oriented. Most households try to grow enough food for their own needs. There may be variation from household to household and from year to year depending upon personnel, rainfall, non-farm income and the management skill of the household head. When drought precludes a successful subsistence harvest, the households may try to fill the gap from the proceeds of their non-farm work and the sale of cash crops. Cash crops consist of beans, ground-nuts and sometimes food grains and are secondary for most farm families. The widespread belief that African rural peoples have been forced to replace food with export crops for the more developed world does not apply in Borno. Cash cropping is in addition to, not in place of, food production.

The biggest change in farm methods is that of fertilizer application. During my first visit to Magumeri in the 1950s local farmers rejected the attempt by the government to have them adopt heavily subsidized fertilizers. In the 1980s almost every farmer had used some, and those that did not said they would do so if more were available.

There are other indications of change. Special development programs aimed at small farmers are now in place and expanding. They provide extension services, widespread selling outlets for fertilizers or even a tractor and driver for those willing to rent one for a few hours. Only a few years after the program began (in 1982), a number of small peasant farmers have expanded into large commercial producers who raise crops for sale in the cities. When we surveyed two regions of the program in 1984 there were 280 farmers (out of 50,000 contacted in some way) that had expanded their acreage from under 5 hectares to over 25. Along the main highways, there are now a few very large commercial farms run by city businessmen who have invested in the rural areas. They have paid to clear new land or have purchased plots from villagers to diversify their interests. The government's policy of helping in the development of commercial farming has stimulated investment. These units are often fenced and mechanized. Billboards along the roads advertise the company and its products: chickens, eggs, meat and traditional food crops. Whether such farms are a threat to small farmers or whether traditional small peasant farming can exist side by side with modern capitalist large-scaled farms is a question for research. Meanwhile it sparks much controversy both inside and outside the country. Many say that Nigeria is heading toward a Latin Americanization of its rural society with a few large landowners and a vast landless peasantry. Others point out that there is as yet no land shortage in Borno or the rest of the country, with the exception of areas around the large cities. Peasants, they say, are oriented to feeding themselves not the growing millions in the cities. Only large scale commercial farming can support that type of production. My present research is aimed at answering this question at least for Borno and hopefully with possible applications in other parts of Africa.

What about the quality of life? Inside the households much is as it always has been. The children are taught the same behavioral norms; local political leaders are still much respected. Religion, ceremonial life, and indeed most of the rhythm of daily life remains recognizable and consistent with earlier description. When I asked a large sample of farmers in rural areas (in 1984) about changes in their quality of life in the last two decades, most of them mentioned transportation as the most significant improvement. My wife and I were startled, at first, to see cattle on their way to market reclining in small Japanese pick-up trucks. Better roads and comfortable vehicles were most often cited as improvements in transportation. Next on the list of significant change was educational opportunities for children. There are more schools, more secondary schools and even a university. People seem to feel that their lives are better today than twenty years ago because of government investments in public services that decrease the drudgery and isolation of earlier times and give them hope for their children. When I wrote this book, the majority of villagers visited the city only on rare occasions, some not at all. Life centered on the village or nearby hamlets and towns where people farmed, visited kin, friends and the local markets. Today everyone can travel to the city easily and often which they do. Almost half of the households have a battery radio where only one or two plus the town reading room had one when we first arrived in the late 1950s. Borno life is still much the same, but it is much more closely linked to that of the city. The national radio network makes local and even world news part of village conversation.

The continuities are also striking. Approaching Magumeri with my wife in 1982 after many years' absence, we were struck by memories and similarities. The separate group of men still reclined under a shade tree in the afternoon sun discussing the affairs of the day. The women carried firewood back to town and gathered around the well for water and spritely conversation before setting off in household groups of straight lines, senior to junior, with water jugs gracefully balanced on one shoulder. People still removed their shoes when approaching the District Head's compound, just as they had thirty years before when I first arrived. Deep respect for the officials of the town was still an honored tradition.

Everywhere we faced the same subtle and extraordinary courtesy. Working with field assistants in 1984, I relished a cool thermos of ice water after a few hours in the dusty heat. The young District Head of Magumeri sent his car and driver to the city for the ice and water because he knew, he said softly, that expatriates drink only treated water. Silently, I compared this with a similar kindness in 1956 in this same village. I was seriously ill with hepatitis and the District Head sent a messenger on horseback who rode all night to the city to fetch a landrover which eventually delivered me to a hospital some 24 hours later. The technology involved had changed but the abiding spirit of concern remained: formal and firm.

The organization of non-farming crafts, especially trade, is still essentially the same. A wealthy official or business man is patron to a number of clients who use household norms of respect and trust to link together in an organization. Greater variety now exists so that gasoline service stations are run by clients as well as small stalls in markets. Hotels, export-import goods, and transportation are now commonly added to these urban enterprises. The very wealthy live in large mansions with their own mosques and fleets of cars. A few are turning traditional enterprises into the beginnings of modern incorporated businesses with boards of directors and diversified holdings. Clients and kin serve as managers of the separate divisions of the business. Banks and law firms are part of the urban economy in a much more ordinary way than was the case when we first arrived. Indeed, there were no law firms in Borno when this book was written. Now there are several, all busy expanding their operations.

In the political realm much has changed. Just under the surface, however, much remains. The structure of Borno Emirate is still as it was. The Shehu is the "traditional ruler" of the emirate. Today he has a telephone in his reception room and a council chamber with a huge conference table. The Waziri has a modern office with clerk typists running back and forth with files amidst the clusters of robed messengers and palace servants. The servants guard the entrances with a wary sleepiness that is immediately halted when an important-looking stranger appears to keep an appointment or to seek an audience. The royal court, the titled hierarchy, and the system of district, village and hamlet heads remains the same. Urban planners from England advised that the system be maintained as the core of city government. Ordinary people were familiar with the system and would be more comfortable when they required public actions to redress wrongs, made complaints, and needed access to the newer forms of local government. It has therefore been continued as part of an expanded and more representative form of municipal and township organization.

As noted in the last few pages, party politics came to Borno in the 1960s. At that time they simply represented a means by which the ruling groups could participate in national politics and maintain local power. In the second period (1979-1983), a new constitution assured much more support for opposition parties. All parties had to show national, not just local, ethnic, or regional support. Borno was won by an "opposition" group that differed from the winners of the national election. Federal and state governments were in the hands of rival political groups. This led to conflict, competition, and benefits. The federal government divided the entire country into River Basin Development Authorities and invested heavily in a huge irrigation scheme around the western (Borno) side of Lake Chad. It is not cost-effective, but the local people are pleased to have received their share of the "national cake."

The most consequential event of recent Nigerian history to affect Borno was the Nigerian civil war and the events that led up to it. Ethnic riots against Igbo peoples in northern Nigeria were at first avoided. The Shehu called local leaders to the palace and ordered them to keep the peace. That was in 1966. A second outbreak in 1967 could not be controlled in northern Nigeria. This was soon followed by the civil war in which Igbo leaders tried to take the peoples of southeastern Nigeria into a secessionist state called "Biafra." Every part of the country was affected. Kanuri men had to fight in the war, the economy was put on a war footing to win and unite the country. Possibly it would have happened anyway, but the conflict forged the nation in a way that nothing has before or since. Even in the remotest Kanuri villages people became aware of and identified with the nation. Before the war, Nigerian identity was vague and limited to an elite few whose lives and careers were absorbed in the national arena.

Ethnicity is still a strong and durable force in Borno and indeed in Nigerian national life. To be a Kanuri, a member of one of the major traditional ethnic groups is meaningful. It may help or hinder one's life chances in important ways. Borno and Kanuri identity are no different in this respect than any other modern nation state. The inflammatory potency of ethnic differences has been permanently diminished and placed under tight controls by the war. Indeed, it is not polite in modern Nigeria to ask someone directly about his or her ethnicity. The questioner may query regarding which part of the country someone comes from and then may make the deductions with a few hints from language usage, personal name, religion, and home town. Increasingly important are new interest groups: labor unions, professional associations, political affiliation, or religion. Such affiliations cut across ethnicity, occupational status, and locality. Nigeria, and indeed Borno, are pluralist societies officially committed to a social and political life that expresses and protects individual and group rights and opportunities.

When I wrote this book in the 1960s, there was not a great deal of contemporary material available. The historical sources were well known and a few interested and scattered scholars referred to them. Today Borno scholarship is expanding exponentially. Local Borno scholars including some Kanuri and expatriates as well, are publishing widely on a variety of topics. A new journal, *Borno Studies*, is available from the University of Maiduguri and a *Borno Bibliography* has been brought out by scholars at the same University. Borno history, linguistics, sociology, geography, agronomy, hydrology, geology, biology, aesthetics, and general development studies are accumulating a literature of their own. As with other parts of the world, Borno research has become compartmentalized into topics and disciplines. Each compares aspects of the area with similar features elsewhere.

What about the future? Hidden causes, unintended consequences of policy implementation, and outside forces produce unknowable outcomes in human affairs. History and society always face uncertain futures. Nevertheless, some general trends are clear. Borno has developed a large urban center whose population will top a million by the end of the century. A string of smaller cities are growing at almost the same rate. In-migration to the cities will continue. Rural development, especially schooling, supports and accelerates this transformation as do widespread attitudes. In our farm survey in 1984, over half of the household heads questionned said they did not want their sons to be farmers! Yet rural areas will remain in many respects the same. They will still be dominated by small peasant farms although they will be different. They will be more productive using modern technology. There will be large commercial farms that produce an expanding proportion of agriculture's yield. The transformation of society that occurred elsewhere along with industrialization has already taken its first steps in Borno. The way forward is unalterable. Kanuri language and culture will survive as long as there are people in villages. The majority still live and will continue to live for the next generation or so in this manner. The heterogeneity of urban life means that the Hausa language will eventually diminish the use of Kanuri in government offices, commerce, and telephone conversations with other parts of the country.

There are dangers as well. The threat of desertification and periodic drought is a constant and must be dealt with through planning and infractructure development. Water management and conservation must prepare for prudent use of the environment. Reforestation is an extreme need which must be addressed. The program carried out in Haiti might serve as a model for future development policy. The short term economic difficulties in the country have produced severe hardships in Borno as elsewhere in the 1980s. Lack of housing, inflation, unemployment, runaway food prices and shortages have meant instability and volatility among the urban poor and even the lower to middle income groups. In Borno, as elsewhere in northern Nigeria, one of the responses has been the rise of Islamic millenarian cults that threaten public order. These are the result of frustration, ignorance, and urban misery. As social control and economic conditions improve and as education provides better explanations of current events, I hope such problems will dissipate.

In the long run, prospects are bright. Borno's very remoteness, its sense of its own rich past and the sophistication of its leaders combined with the dynamism of Nigeria as a modern nation means that real and irreversible progress should be assured.

Recommended Reading

General Reading on the Culture Area

HODGKIN, T. L., 1960, *Nigerian Perspectives; An Historical Anthology*. London: Oxford University Press.

> A useful introduction to many of the historical writings on Nigerian societies, especially the northern emirates. The author also synthesizes the material into a general historical summary of the western Sudan.

HOGBEN, S. J., 1930, *The Muhammadan Emirates of Northern Nigeria*. London: Oxford University Press.

> Brief summaries of the emirates of northern Nigeria and their place in the history of the western Sudan.

HOPEN, C. E., 1958, *The Pastoral Fulbe Family in Gwandu*. London: Oxford University Press.

> A general account of Fulani family life in a semi-sedentary population to the west of Bornu.

MEEK, C. K., 1925, *The Northern Tribes of Nigeria*. London: Oxford University Press.

> A most comprehensive description of the range of cultures to be found in northern Nigeria.

NADEL, S. F., 1946, *A Black Byzantium*. London: Oxford University Press.

> A detailed description and analysis of the Nupe emirate to the west of Bornu which was more recently Islamized and has many interesting similiarities and differences to the social and political system of Bornu. This author has also published a book on Nupe religion.

SMITH, M. F., 1955, *Baba of Karo, A Woman of the Muslim Hausa*. London: Faber and Faber; New York: Praeger, 1964.

> The life story of a woman of northern Nigeria giving sensitive insight into the women's position in this area as it is, and was, during the last sixty years.

SMITH, M. G., 1960, *Government in Zazzau, 1800–1950*. London: Oxford University Press.

> A detailed historical and social anthropological analysis of the emirate system of government as it has spanned the last century and a half in Hausaland. The author has also written extensively on local economic life among the Hausa in Zaria Province.

STENNING, D. J., 1959, *Savannah Nomads*. London: Oxford University Press.
An excellent report on the social life of the Fulani semi-sedentary nomads of Bornu and the way in which they relate to the way of life of the settled Kanuri.

TRIMINGHAM, H. S., 1959, *Islam in West Africa*. London: Oxford University Press.
A detailed working out of the way in which Islam has been received in West Africa and the changes it has effected in the area.

Specific References to the Kanuri

BARTH, H., 1857, *Travels and Discoveries in North and Central Africa*. London: Longmans, 5 vols.
A detailed description of Bornu and the western Sudan in the 1850s by one of the most painstaking observers and explorers of nineteenth century Africa. This work also includes the first published account in English of Bornu history.

BENTON, P. A., 1913, *The Sultanate of Bornu; Translated From the German of Dr. A. Schultze with Additions and Appendices*. London: Oxford University Press.
One of the few earlier works that describes the culture of the Kanuri, although rather briefly and unsystematically. There are also a number of interesting documents added by Benton that deal with the beginnings of the second dynasty in the early nineteenth century.

BOAHEN, A. A., 1964, *Britain, the Sahara, and the Western Sudan, 1788–1861*. Oxford, England: Clarendon Press.
An account by an acute historical observer of the effects of British influence in an early period of western Sudanic history.

COHEN, R., 1961, "Marriage Instability Among the Kanuri of Northern Nigeria," *American Anthropologist*, Vol. 63, 1231–1249.
An analysis of the factors causing high divorce among the Kanuri.

———, 1964, "Conflict and Change in a Northern Nigerian Emirate," *in* Zollschan, G., and D. Hirsch (eds.), *Explorations in Social Change*. Boston: Houghton Mifflin.
A summary and analysis of the problems associated with the role of the district head in Bornu.

———, 1965, "Institutionalized Exchange: A Kanuri Example," *Cahiers d'Etudes Africaines*, Vol. 5, 353–369.
A discussion of traditional Kanuri concepts of money and their relation to the social system, especially superior-subordinate relationships.

———, 1966, "The Dynamics of Feudalism in Bornu," *Boston University Publications on Africa*, Vol. 2, *African History*, Butler, Jeffrey (ed.), 87-105.
An attempt to analyze the longevity of Kanuri political institutions and explain their durability in comparison to feudal forms of government elsewhere.

———, 1966, "From Empire to Colony: Bornu in the 19th and 20th Centuries," *in* Turner, V. (ed.) *The Impact of Colonialism*, Stanford: Hoover Institute, (in press).
An historical account of the political system of nineteenth century Bornu and